kids'
kitchen

MITCHELL BEAZLEY

Kids' Kitchen
Good food made easy

First published in Great Britain in 2005 by Mitchell Beazley, an imprint of Octopus Publishing Group Limited, 2–4 Heron Quays, London E14 4JP.

This paperback edition published in 2007 by Mitchell Beazley.

Distributed in the United States and Canada by Sterling Publishing Co., Inc., 387 Park Avenue South, New York, NY 10016–8810

A CIP catalogue record for this book is available from the British Library.

ISBN-13: 978 1 84533 316 4
ISBN-10: 1 84533 316 0

While all reasonable care has been taken during the preparation of this edition, neither the publisher, editors, nor the authors can accept responsibility for any consequences arising from the use thereof or from the information contained therein.

Commissioning Editors: Vivien Antwi and Rebecca Spry
Executive Art Editor: Yasia Williams
Design: Tim Pattinson
Editors: Vanessa Kendell and Rebecca Spry
Home Economy Assistant: Sibilla Whitehead
Photography: Francesca Yorke
Production: Seyhan Esen
Index: John Noble

Colour reproduction by Bright Arts

Printed and bound by Toppan Printing Company in China

For Ella, Jasmin and Finn X

Thanks Becca, this is the book I have always wanted to write, you are truly wonderful to work with. Thanks David for believing in everything I do. Pop, you and mummy gave me a brilliant childhood—for that I will always be grateful. Thanks for always being there.

Vicki, you star for introducing me to Becca, I do miss seeing you. To all my friends, especially Billy, for all your tireless help; Amanda, Annie, Kate, Liz, and Lou for testing recipes, recipe ideas, and just listening. Milly, thanks for your recipe testing, and I hope you continue to enjoy cooking the recipes with your friends.

Fran, what can I say, a photo shoot I will never forget! A huge thank you to you for the totally gorgeous pictures. Thanks to Tim and Yasia—it really does look fantastic.

A big thank you to all the local "amateur" models—Alice, Archie, Bea, Charlie, Edward, Ella, Emily, Jack, Jacob, Jake, Jasmin, Kirsty, Lucia, Rosa, Tamas, Teddy, Tilly, William, Zoe, and to all the models from Alphabet Kidz—Iman, Louis, Mae, Morgan, and Usman—you really have helped make this book come to life, well done to all of you!

Diona, Vivien and Vanessa, phew—thanks for all your stirling efforts.

Finally, a quick thanks to my local stores for helping me cook good food, especially to Bill and his team at Bill's Food Store; all the guys (and Petrina) at Frank Richards Butcher's; and Vera and Arran at the Lewes Fruit Store.

7/07

kids'
kitchen

6 introduction and good kitchen practice

introduction

for mom and dad

I am totally passionate about getting children into the kitchen. They need to be able to get messy with food, to touch, smell and learn about food, and one of the best ways to do this is to let them cook. This does not have to mean that your children spend hours baking, leaving behind a wake of destruction. It can be that they just start by helping you with simple tasks, such as crushing garlic or beating egg whites. My youngest is eighteen months and he loves to hold the electric hand mixer with me when I am beating egg whites, although I am sure it is the noise from the mixer that excites him more than anything else!

However, learning about food does not just involve cooking, it also means having an understanding of where food comes from.

This book is for children, it is their recipe book to keep, use, and refer to over and over. Once they have mastered some of the basic techniques explained here, they will be able to cook good food pretty much anywhere. If children are given the chance to try making food for themselves and their family or friends, they are also more likely to enjoy eating a wide variety of foods.

for you

I have been involved with good food for as long as I can remember. My mother was an excellent cook and she enthused about really good quality food and the joy of cooking for family and friends. I loved cooking from a very young age and by the grand old age of six I was selling cakes to my mother's friends for extra pocket money.

I remember being allowed to collect fresh eggs from the hens on our local farm and being so excited when we cooked them for breakfast. Have you ever been to a farm? If not, ask your mom or dad if you could go to see the animals and chickens, or visit a working dairy to see the cows being milked. Don't be afraid to ask questions, such as how many eggs hens lay, or what they eat, or what happens to the milk once it leaves the dairy.

Farmers' markets are also a great way to learn about food and what we eat. The people selling the food are often the people who produce it, so you will find that they knows a lot about their produce.

A big part of my childhood was spent shopping for food at our local butcher store, bakery, fruitstore and fish store, from whom I learned a great deal about where food comes from. Shopping, whether it is in a supermarket or local food store, is a big part of our every day life, so try to enjoy it. Even your younger brothers or sisters can have fun going to get things off the shelves and putting them into the cart or counting out fruit and vegetables into bags. Ask your mom or dad if you can be given the responsibility of choosing food, such as a cut of meat or some fresh fish.

Once you have helped to shop for your food, you can think about cooking. Just as when you started to read you learned the sound of letters before putting them together to make words, when you start to cook it is a good idea to learn some of the basic techniques first, which you can then use to make a whole variety of dishes. For example, once you know how to beat egg whites, you can make meringues, fruit fools, and chocolate mousse. Learning how to rub butter into flour means you can make pastry as well as cookies and crumble toppings.

There are so many skills to learn in this book, but most importantly, have fun in the kitchen and enjoy eating—and sharing—the good food that you have made.

good kitchen practice

GETTING STUCK IN

Before you get stuck in, have a quick read through the following and check with your mom or dad that it is OK for you to do some cooking. Read the recipes before you start and try to get all your ingredients measured out and your equipment ready. You will find it easier when you start cooking, and you can always pretend to be a professional chef—with everything ready to hand! When I was eight years old, I used to make my brothers sit and watch me cook so that I could pretend to be on television!

MEASURING CUPS

The recipes in this book use cup measures. Measuring cups come in different sizes, or are sometimes adjusted using a slide bar to measure different amounts. They can be used to measure dry ingredients. Glass or clear plastic containers with a pour spout and handle can be used to measure liquid ingredients, and have the cup measures marked on the side.

SPOONS

If possible, try to use measuring teaspoons and tablespoons, which are available from large supermarkets or good cookware stores. A heaped spoon can contain double the amount of a level spoon, so keep an eye on this—it's especially important if you are baking.

EQUIPMENT

Hopefully you will have most things needed for the recipes in your kitchen already, and I am sure that in most cases you can improvise if you do not have the exact thing. A hand blender is a particularly useful piece of equipment. They do not cost a lot of money and you can use them for many different things, such as smoothies, soups, and fruit purées to mix with yogurt. A vegetable peeler with an easy-to-grip handle is also very useful.

OVEN

You may have noticed that there are many different types of oven. Some have gas hobs (the top of the oven where you rest the saucepan, skillet, etc) and others are electric. Some ovens are gas and similarly, others are electric. Most electric ovens have a little red light that goes out when the oven is at the right temperature. The more cooking you do, the more you will get to know how your oven works. You may need to vary the cooking time slightly to suit your oven—some ovens cook food more quickly than others and your food may be cooked in 15 minutes even if the recipe says 20.

You will need to check your food before the recommended cooking time is up just in case it is cooking quickly. Remember to turn your oven on 10–15 minutes before you need it because it can take a little while to warm up, and remember to turn it off when you have finished.

A WORD ON SAFETY

To stay safe in the kitchen, please spend 5 minutes reading through this section.

- Knives and the blades of blenders and food processors are sharp. Always check with your mom or dad before using them and handle them very carefully.
- Ovens, broilers and hobs can get very hot —always wear oven gloves when you are putting things into the oven or broiler or taking them out.
- Be careful when you are stirring hot things in pans. Keep your hands, arms and face a safe distance away from boiling water or steam.
- Keep paper towels or dish towels away from the hob.
- If you drop anything on the floor pick it up and wipe it up to prevent anyone from slipping on it.
- Turn pan handles to the side of the stove that the pans don't get knocked off the hob.
- Always ask your mom or dad to help you carry heavy pans or tip food into a colander or serving dish.

A WORD ON HYGIENE

- Slip an apron on before you begin—not only does this stop you from getting your clothes all covered in food, but it stops any dirt, paint, etc from falling off your clothes and into your food.
- Wash your hands before you start cooking.
- Tie back your hair if it is long.
- Try to use different chopping boards for different foods—for example, keep one for meats, one for fruit and vegetables, etc. If this is not possible, please wash them thoroughly in-between jobs.
- Make sure that the ingredients you use are within their "use by"date.
- Only reheat cooked foods once and make sure they are piping hot all the way through to the middle.

A FEW FINAL THINGS

Look after your kitchen—put hot dishes, straight from the oven, on to mats so that you do not damage your work surface. Clear up when you have finished—it can be fun washing everything down with a cloth and soapy water!

1 FROM THE SEA

pan-frying fish

Pan-frying, or frying in the minimum of fat, is suitable for a variety of fish, particularly white fish, such as flounder, sole, cod, bass, and haddock and some oily fish, such as salmon, trout ,and mackerel. Frying in butter gives fish a lovely flavor, but butter burns easily. Mixing butter with oil enables you to heat it to a higher temperature. You can pan-fry fillets of fish or smaller whole fish.

flounder with herb butter

SERVES 4

YOU WILL NEED:
INGREDIENTS
- ½ stick butter, softened
- 2 tablespoons parsley, finely chopped
- a large pinch of salt and freshly ground black pepper
- 4 thin fillets white fish, such as flounder
- 2 tablespoons all-purpose flour
- 2 tablespoons olive oil
- lemon wedges, to serve

EQUIPMENT
- bowl
- small wooden spoon
- waxed paper
- knife
- 2 large plates
- large skillet
- fish turner

1   Put half of the butter in a bowl and, using a small wooden spoon, beat until soft. Mix in the parsley and a pinch of salt and pepper.

2   Scoop the butter on to a piece of waxed paper. Fold the paper tightly over the butter and roll it into a sausage shape. Put the butter in the refrigerator.

3   Unless your fish is boneless, run your finger over it to check for bones. If you find any, cut them out with a knife.

4   Put the flour on to a plate and mix in a pinch of salt and pepper. Dip each fillet in the flour and shake off the excess. Put the fillets on a clean plate.

5   Heat the oil and remaining butter in a frying pan until it starts to bubble. Pan-fry the fish 3–4 minutes, (A) then turn with a fish turner (don't move the fish before this time; it may have stuck to the pan) and fry a further 3–4 minutes, depending on the thickness of your fish, until cooked. When fish is cooked it changes from transparent to white, the flesh is firmer, it flakes easily, and the edges should be turning pale golden brown.

6   Using a fish turner, lift each piece of fish on to a warm plate. Cut the butter log into eight slices and put two slices on top of each piece of fish. Serve with lemon wedges.

shallow-frying fish

Shallow-frying uses more fat than pan-frying, and oil is used instead of a combination of oil and butter. The skillet is filled with about ½ inch of oil. White fish, such as flounder, haddock, and cod, or little oily fish. such as sardines and herrings, are often shallow fried. The fish tends to be cut into bite-size pieces or small fillets before frying, but you can use tiny whole fish. The fish is coated in seasoned flour, then beaten egg, and then dipped in breadcrumbs, oatmeal, or polenta. This protects the flesh from the heat and gives it a lovely crisp coating. The best oil to use is something flavorless, such as canola oil.

to shallow-fry fish:

1   Pour the oil into a skillet— it should be about ½ inch deep.

2   Put the pan over a medium heat. The oil needs to be quite hot so that the outside of the fish gets crisp and golden but the inside is less well cooked. To test the oil, drop a small cube of bread into it Ⓐ — if it sizzles, you know the oil is ready.

3   Spread your seasoned flour on a plate, put your beaten egg in a shallow bowl, and put some breadcrumbs (see page 25) on a plate.

4   Rinse the boneless fish under cold water. Put it on to paper towels and pat dry. If you are cooking a fish fillet, cut it in half lengthwise.

5   Dip the fish first in the seasoned flour and shake off any excess, then in the beaten egg before letting any excess drip back into the bowl, then in the breadcrumbs, using your hands to sprinkle the crumbs over it so it is completely covered.

6   Using a fish turner, add the fish to the pan. Cook 3–4 minutes, depending on its thickness, then use a fish turner to gently turn it and cook until it is golden all over. You can cook more than one fillet half at a time if there is room in your pan.

7   Lift the fish out using a fish turner and put it on to a plate lined with kitchen towels, which will absorb any excess oil. Cover with foil to keep warm.

8   Cook the remaining fish in batches. Serve with lemon wedges.

shallow-frying fish

Adding a little lemon zest to the breadcrumb coating helps to bring out the flavour of the fish. Try serving these fish sticks with some mayonnaise mixed with a little lemon juice.

lemony fish sticks

MAKES APPROX 16 (APPROX 4 SERVINGS)

YOU WILL NEED:
INGREDIENTS
- 6 tablespoons all-purpose flour
- a pinch of salt and freshly ground black pepper
- very finely grated zest of ½ lemon
- 1 large egg
- 1 tablespoons cold water
- 1 cup dried breadcrumbs (see page 25)
- 1 lb boneless white fish fillets, such as cod or haddock
- ⅔–1 cup canola oil
- a small cube of bread

EQUIPMENT
- lemon zester
- 4 large plates
- shallow bowl
- fork
- kitchen towels
- knife
- chopping board
- skillet
- slotted spoon

1 Put the flour on to a plate and mix in a pinch of salt and pepper and the lemon zest. Crack the egg by tapping it firmly against the side of a shallow bowl, pushing your thumbs into the crack and carefully pulling the shell apart, letting the egg drop into the bowl. Add the water and beat well with a fork. Put the breadcrumbs on a plate.

2 Check the fish for bones and pat dry with kitchen towels.

3 Using a knife and a chopping board, cut the fish into strips as thick as your thumb but a little longer.

4 Dip a piece of fish into the flour, then the egg, then the breadcrumbs (see page 13, point 5). Lay on a clean plate.

5 Do the same with all the other pieces of fish—once you get going you can do a few at a time so it doesn't take too long. Wash and dry your hands.

6 Ⓐ Shallow-fry the fish until cooked (see page 13, points 6–8). Eat immediately.

roasting fish

Roasting—cooking in the oven with a little fat—is a quick and easy way to cook fish. The oven is turned on to a high setting so that the fish cooks quickly, keeping the flesh moist. But the high heat can dry out the flesh, so it is best to use thicker fish, such as salmon, cod, bass, and haddock, and be careful not to overcook it. To keep the fish moist, a little fat is added—a drizzle of olive oil or a few dots of butter. Unless you want the fish to have a crisp crust, like the recipe below, cover your roasting dish with a piece of foil before putting it in the oven.

roast salmon with an orange crust

SERVES 4

YOU WILL NEED:

INGREDIENTS
- approx 1 tablespoon olive oil
- 4 boneless salmon fillets, approx 1 inch thick
- a large pinch of salt and freshly ground black pepper
- ½ stick butter, melted
- 4 tablespoons breadcrumbs (see page 25)
- a handful of chopped fresh herbs, such as parsley, rosemary, and dill
- zest of ½ orange

EQUIPMENT
- lemon zester
- baking tray
- pastry brush
- small bowl
- oven gloves
- fish turner

1   Turn the oven on to 425°F.

2   Pour the oil into a baking sheet and use a pastry brush to spread it all over —this helps to stop the fish sticking to the sheet. Wash the fish.

3   Put the fish on the baking sheet and season with a pinch of salt and pepper. Ⓐ Brush each fillet with melted butter.

4   Put the breadcrumbs in a small bowl. Using your fingers, mix in the herbs, orange zest, and a pinch of salt and pepper. Ⓑ Sprinkle the breadcrumbs evenly over the fish fillets.

5   Using oven gloves, put the baking sheet in the oven and roast 10–12 minutes. The fish should be firm and it should have turned from almost transparent to not transparent. (If your fish fillets are 2 inches thick they will need more than twice as long to cook, i.e. 20–25 minutes.) It is important not to overcook the fish because it will dry out.

6   Using oven gloves, take the baking sheet out of the oven. Use a fish turner to lift the fish off the baking sheet on to four plates. Eat immediately.

roasting fish

A kebab is made up of small pieces of fish, meat, or vegetables threaded on to skewers, which are then roasted, broiled, griddled, or barbecued. You can use metal skewers or wooden skewers that have been soaked in water to stop them from burning. Fish with a firm, meaty texture, such as cod and monkfish, and oily fish, such as salmon, tuna, swordfish, and mackerel, are ideal for kebabs. Fish is often marinated in herbs and spices before being cooked, but it should only be marinated for a short time because its tender flesh absorbs the flavors quickly. If you leave fish in a marinade that contains lots of an acidic ingredient, such as wine or lemon juice, it will start to cook the fish.

cod and crunchy pesto bread kebabs

MAKES 14 SMALL KEBABS (ENOUGH FOR A FAMILY OF 4)

YOU WILL NEED:

INGREDIENTS
- 1lb cod fillet
- 1 small ciabatta loaf
- 4 tablespoons pesto
- 2 tablespoons olive oil
- 28 cherry tomatoes
- a little extra oil, for drizzling

EQUIPMENT
- knife
- 2 chopping boards
- serrated knife
- large bowl
- 14 wooden kebab sticks (approx 7 inches long) soaked in water for at least 30 minutes
- roasting pan
- oven gloves

1 Turn the oven on to 425°F.

2 **A** Unless your fish is boneless, run your finger over it to check for bones. If you find any, cut them out with a knife. Cut the fish into 1 inch pieces.

3 On another chopping board, use a serrated knife to cut the bread into 42 cubes about the same size as the fish. Put the bread in a bowl and add the pesto and olive oil. **B** Using your hands, mix together so that all the bread is covered in pesto.

4 Take a wooden skewer and thread a piece of fish on to it, then a piece of bread, then a tomato. Continue until there are three pieces each of bread and fish and two tomatoes on each kebab. Lay the kebabs in the roasting pan. Drizzle a little extra oil over the kebabs.

5 Using oven gloves put the pan in the oven and roast 10–14 minutes. Using oven gloves, take the pan out of the oven and serve.

roasting shellfish

There are many types of shellfish, for instance crabs, mussels, and shrimp. They taste wonderful, but some people find them too fiddly to prepare and eat. You can now buy many types of shellfish from fish stores or supermarkets ready prepared, so all the hard work has been done for you. This is my eldest daughter Ella's favorite supper.

roast jumbo shrimp in garlic butter

SERVES 4

YOU WILL NEED:

INGREDIENTS
- 4 medium potatoes
- ½ stick unsalted butter, softened
- 2 large garlic cloves, peeled
- a small handful of fresh parsley, chopped
- a pinch of coarse salt and freshly ground black pepper
- 14 oz ready-cooked frozen jumbo shrimp, defrosted

EQUIPMENT
- vegetable scrubbing brush
- knife
- fork
- oven gloves
- small bowl
- garlic press
- metal spoon
- ovenproof dish
- large spoon

1 Turn the oven on to 400°F.

2 Use a brush to scrub the potatoes under cold running water. Remove any potato eyes and use a knife to cut out any obvious bad bits or green bits. Use a fork to prick the potatoes a couple of times. Using oven gloves, put the potatoes into the oven to cook 1 hour.

3 Meanwhile, put the soft butter into a small bowl. Crush the garlic in a garlic press and use a metal spoon to mix it into the butter. Add the parsley, salt, and pepper, and mix well.

4 Put the jumbo shrimp into an ovenproof dish and put blobs of garlic butter all over the top.

5 When the potatoes have 7 minutes cooking time left, use oven gloves to put the jumbo shrimp in the oven.

6 When the potatoes and jumbo shrimp are cooked, use oven gloves to take them out of the oven.

7 Keeping one oven glove on and holding a knife in your other hand, use the knife to cut a cross in the top of the potato. Push the sides of the potato together to open it up. Repeat with the other potatoes.

8 Put each potato on a dinner plate and, using a large spoon, divide the jumbo shrimp among the potatoes. Serve immediately.

what to find by the sea

The seashore is the place where the sea meets the land. It is the area of land or beach that lies in between the high tide and low tide marks. At high tide the top of the beach is covered by the sea and when the tide goes out, at low tide, this same land is visible to the eye.

When it is low tide, the upper part of the beach dries out and any pools of water left behind can get very salty. The temperature on the shore and in the water can change quite dramatically—any living plants and animals have to be very adaptable in order to survive.

When you are next on a beach, look for any rock pools. Rock pools are a great place to find living creatures. Each rock pool is likely to have its own community of animals. In the rock pools found in the middle or at the top of the beach you are likely to see a variety of seaweed. This provides shade for the animals living underneath it and a place for animals to hide from predators such as seagulls.

Under the seaweed and attached firmly to the rocks you will see limpets, periwinkles, and barnacles. These all have strong shells to protect them from the waves and the drying effect of the wind, and strong muscles to grip the rock. They also have to be tough and strong to help protect them from being bashed off by big crashing waves.

Closer to the sea, limpets can often be found attached to the rocks. I remember my father telling me that if you want to get a limpet away from the rock you need to quickly tap it with a piece of driftwood. If you touch the limpet first, it will stick like glue to the rock and will be almost impossible to release. It is also fun to look for periwinkles—you can collect them, but always put them back on the rocks before you go home. You will notice big clusters of mussels attached to the rocks. These are popular cooked with wine, herbs, and garlic in France, although I wouldn't advise cooking mussels found on a beach. Crabs and shrimp survive by hiding in crevices. Buy a cheap fishing net or do as my brothers did and use a piece of netting wrapped around sticks.

On the lower part of the beach—the area nearest the low tide mark—where the beach is wetter you are more likely to find sea anemones, starfish, and seas urchins that all live among the wet seaweeds in the rock pools. You may also be lucky enough to spot some little fish such as blennies. These are not edible, but make a great find.

While you are at the seashore, see if you can find out about any local fishermen and ask them what they have caught that day. You may be in luck and they may offer to sell you some freshly caught fish, which you could cook for your supper.

how to tell if fish is fresh

Just because the fish counter says "fresh fish for sale," it does not actually guarantee that the fish is "fresh." Fish found on some fish counters may have been out of the water for an outrageous two weeks. It could have been chilled on a trawler for a week and then spent a number of days in distribution. Fish that has been kept for this long will

not harm you, as long as it has been kept chilled, but neither will it taste that great.

However, there are many fish stores where they take real pride in how quickly they can get fresh fish from sea to shop. When you next go to choose fish, take a long look at it before you buy. To help you decide whether it is fresh and whether it will taste good, think about the following. Whatever happens, don't be shy or embarrassed about taking a good look or asking questions; if they are proud of their fish they should not be concerned about your curiosity. The fish should have clear and bright eyes. The gills under the flaps on either side of the head should be bright red, because this indicates the presence of oxygen—gills stay red for up to four days. The flesh should be firm. Touch the fish with your finger—the pressure should not mark the fish and the flesh should spring back to normal. The skin should look slimy and feel slippery. The fish should have a healthy sea smell, not an ammonia smell, which is a sign of an old fish.

smoking fish

Smoking is a way of preserving food, so that it can be kept for longer without going off—although, of course, it still needs to be used before the "use by" date on the package. Smoked fish also takes on a lovely smoky flavour. Smoked haddock and cod need to be cooked before you can eat them, but some smoked fish, such as smoked salmon, can be very thinly sliced and eaten as they are.

smoked haddock kedgeree

SERVES 4

YOU WILL NEED:
INGREDIENTS
- 1 lb undyed boneless smoked haddock fillets
- 1 cup whole milk milk
- 1 cup cold water
- 1 cup long-grain rice
- 3 hard-boiled eggs (see page 50)
- ½ stick butter
- a handful of fresh parsley, chopped
- a pinch of salt and freshly ground black pepper

EQUIPMENT
- shallow saucepan or deep skillet
- medium saucepan
- colander
- slotted spoon
- plate
- knife
- large skillet
- wooden spoon

1 Wash the fish, put it in a shallow saucepan or deep skillet and pour over the milk and cold water. Slowly bring to a boil, watching all the time because milk can boil over very quickly. As soon as it bubbles, turn the heat down and cook the fish gently 8–10 minutes (see page 24) until cooked. Remove from the heat.

2 Fill a medium saucepan three-quarters full with cold water. Bring to a boil, add the rice, and cook 12 minutes. Take the pan to the sink and drain the rice in a colander.

3 Lift the fish out of the pan using a slotted spoon and put on a plate. Flake the fish into big pieces using your fingers, removing any bits of skin. You can discard the poaching liquid.

4 Peel the eggs and cut each one into eight wedges. Melt the butter in a large skillet. Add the rice, fish, eggs, and parsley. Stir gently with a wooden spoon over a medium heat until heated through. Taste and add a pinch of salt and pepper. Serve immediately.

poaching fish

Poaching is one of the best ways to cook fish because it cooks food gently and keeps the delicate flesh moist. The fish is placed in a pan, covered with liquid, and cooked over a very low heat or in a very low oven. Poaching is also healthy, because you don't need to use any fat. There are several liquids you can use to poach fish: wine or hard cider, milk or a mixture of milk and water, or fish or vegetable stock. Whichever is used, it is often flavored by adding herbs, finely sliced vegetables, such as onions or carrots, lemon juice and spices, such as bay leaves and peppercorns.

White fish, such as cod and haddock, is often poached in milk. The milk can then be used to flavour a sauce, which can make up part of the finished dish. For example, you can strain the poaching liquid and use it to make a white sauce with finely chopped parsley, which you can serve with fish cakes or as the base for a fish pie.

Smoked fish, such as smoked haddock, is often poached in a mixture of milk and water—for example for kedgeree (see page 22). This helps to reduce the smokiness, which can otherwise be a bit overpowering.

Some fish, such as trout or salmon, are delicious poached whole because this keeps the flesh moist, and they are then good served cold. A whole cleaned, scaled, and gutted fish is put in a large pan and covered in water or fish stock. Often vegetables are added to give a subtle flavour to the fish. It is cooked gently, the liquid barely simmering, and is then left to cool off in the liquid. Cold poached fish is often served with a flavored mayonnaise or other sauce.

Plain fillets, such as flounder or sole, are sometimes poached in wine or hard cider and served with a creamy sauce made with some of the poaching liquid.

to poach a piece of fish for a pie or fish cakes:

1 Run your fingers over the fish fillet to check for bones (unless you are using a boneless fillet). If you find any, cut them out with a knife. Wash the fish and put it skin side down into a shallow saucepan or deep skillet.

2 Pour over enough poaching liquid to cover the fish and add any herbs you are using, such as bay leaves or parsley stalks, to the pan.

3 Ⓐ Very slowly bring up to simmering point, watching carefully, especially if you are using milk. Ask an adult to help you if necessary.

4 As soon as the liquid bubbles, turn the heat down. and cook the fish very gently 5 minutes—the surface should be wobbling rather than bubbling. If the fish is very thick, you may need to cook it a minute or 2 longer. When the fish is cooked, the flesh turns from almost transparent to a much denser color and will feel firmer.

5 Remove from the heat and leave to cool. Lift the fish out of the pan on to a plate using a fish turner. Flake the fish into big pieces using your fingers, removing any bits of skin or bones.

breadcrumbing fish

Fish is often coated in breadcrumbs before cooking, especially if it is going to be shallow-fried or deep-fried. Breadcrumbs protect the fish's delicate flesh from the high heat, seal in the juices, and help to prevent overcooking. The coating also gives the fish a crispy outer layer, which is a great contrast to the soft fish inside.

When fish is breadcrumbed, the crumbs should always be stale and/or dried out in the oven. Dry crumbs will not spit when they go into hot fat and they will absorb less fat than fresh crumbs, making the coating crispier. If you are pan-frying, your fish will only need a very thin layer of breadcrumb coating, but if you are shallow-frying or deep-frying the fish needs to be completely sealed.

To coat the fish, spread some flour mixed with a pinch of salt and pepper on a plate or in a shallow bowl and put some breadcrumbs on another plate. Beat an egg in a shallow bowl. Pat your fish dry on paper towels. **A** Dip the fish into the flour and shake off any excess. **B** Then dip it into the egg and let the excess drip off. Then dip it into the breadcrumbs, turning it over and using your other hand to sprinkle crumbs over the fish so that it is covered. Lay it on a plate ready to cook.

Breadcrumbs store well either in an airtight container or in a sealed container in the freezer.

to make breadcrumbs:

1 Tear the bread into small pieces. Process them in a food processor until you have fine breadcrumbs—you may need to stop the processor and push down any large bits of bread that have got stuck around the blade, but be careful because the blade is very sharp. Process again until the crumbs are fine and there are no big lumps.

2 Carefully remove the blade and tip the crumbs out into a bowl. If you need fresh breadcrumbs, to put into stuffing for example, this is all you need to do.

3 If you are breadcrumbing fish, turn the oven on to 300°F. Spread the crumbs out evenly in a roasting pan. Using oven gloves, put the pan into the oven and cook for 10 minutes. Using oven gloves, remove from the oven and mix the crumbs around with a wooden spoon so they dry out evenly. Put them back in the oven for another 10 minutes. They should be crisp and a very pale gold when they are done. Cool then store in an airtight container.

breadcrumbing fish

Making fish cakes is a great way to use lots of simple techniques you have already learnt: boiling and mashing potatoes, poaching fish, breadcrumbing, and frying.

cod fish cakes

MAKES 8 SMALL FISH CAKES

YOU WILL NEED:
INGREDIENTS
- 1 lb old potatoes, peeled and cut into quarters
- ½ stick butter
- 2 ¼ cups whole milk
- 14 oz boneless cod fillets, skinned
- a large handful of fresh parsley, chopped
- a large pinch of coarse salt and freshly ground black pepper
- ½ cup all-purpose flour
- ¾ cup fine breadcrumbs (see page 25)
- 2 eggs
- a little oil, for frying
- lemon wedges, to serve

EQUIPMENT
- vegetable peeler
- knife
- chopping board
- 2 medium saucepans
- colander and potato masher
- fish turner
- 5 plates
- wooden spoon
- shallow bowl and fork
- skillet and paper towels

GOOD THINGS TO ADD TO YOUR FISH CAKES
✔ 1–2 tablespoons pesto or tomato ketchup
✔ chopped herbs, such as basil or coriander
✔ chopped olives or capers
✔ different fish: if you are short on time try using tinned tuna or chopped cooked prawns, if you like a smoky flavour use poached smoked haddock

1 Boil the potatoes in a saucepan until tender. Drain in a colander and mash with half of the butter and 3 tablespoons of the milk (see page 96).

2 Wash the fish and put it into a saucepan. Pour over the remaining milk, then slowly bring to simmering point, watching all the time. As soon as it bubbles, turn the heat down, and cook the fish gently 5 minutes until cooked—if the fish is very thick you may need to cook it for a minute longer (see page 24, point 4).

3 Remove from the heat and leave to cool. Using a fish turner, lift the fish out of the pan and put it on a plate. Flake the fish into big pieces using your fingers, removing any bits of skin.

4 Mix the fish into the mashed potato and stir in the parsley and a pinch of salt and pepper.

5 Put the flour on to a plate and mix in a pinch of salt and pepper. Put the breadcrumbs on to another plate. Crack the eggs into a shallow bowl and beat well with a fork.

6 Wash and dry your hands well. Divide the potato mixture into 8 portions and roll each one into a ball. Flatten each portion gently into a round fish cake.

7 Turn each fish cake in the flour to coat, then dip in the beaten eggs and then in the breadcrumbs, making sure they are completely covered (see page 25). Lay the fish cakes on a clean plate ready to cook while you finish coating the rest. Wash your hands.

8 Melt the remaining butter with the oil in a skillet and heat until the butter starts to bubble. Add 4 fish cakes and cook 2–3 minutes. Use a fish turner to turn the fish cakes over, and cook on the other side r another 2–3 minutes. Remove from the pan and keep warm on a plate lined with paper towels while you cook the rest.

cutting meat

Knowing how to cut meat is an important skill. Make sure you use a sharp knife; there is more chance of the knife slipping if you use a blunt one. Always cut meat on a wooden or plastic surface and hold the knife firmly, with the blade pointing away from you. Cut away from your hands and body so that if the knife does slip you won't cut yourself. All cuts of meat are different. Some, such as chicken breasts, are fairly easy to cut. Others, such as stewing meat, are tougher and can be hard to chop. If you do come across bone or sinew, don't force it; just try cutting in a different place.

crispy Mexican chicken nuggets

SERVES 4

YOU WILL NEED:
INGREDIENTS
- 1 stick softened butter, plus a small piece for greasing pan
- 1 garlic clove, peeled and crushed
- 2 ½ tablespoons barbecue sauce
- pinch of freshly ground black pepper
- 6 oz lightly salted plain tortilla chips
- 3 boneless skinless chicken breasts
- a little oil, for greasing

EQUIPMENT
- large roasting pan
- small bowl
- small wooden spoon
- garlic press
- plastic sandwich bag
- rolling pin
- large plate
- chopping board
- 2 knives
- paper towels
- oven gloves

1 Turn the oven on to 350°F. Rub a little butter on to a large roasting tin. Put the stick of butter into a small bowl and beat well with a wooden spoon until soft. Beat in the crushed garlic, barbecue sauce, and pepper.

2 Put the tortilla chips into a plastic sandwich bag, seal, and bash with a rolling pin. When the chips are crushed, tip them out on to a large plate.

3 Put the chicken breasts on to a chopping board (for hygiene, keep one board for chopping meat and fish and a different board for fruit and vegetables—never cut raw and cooked food on the same board). **A** Using a knife, cut each breast in half lengthwise and then cut each half to into thin strips.

4 Lay the strips of chicken on paper towels and pat them dry. Mix the chicken in with the butter until the chicken is covered.

5 **B** Dip a few buttery strips of chicken into the crushed chips. Turn each strip over, pressing down so the chicken is evenly coated in chips. Lay the coated chicken in the roasting pan in a single layer. Repeat with the remaining strips of chicken. Sprinkle any remaining chips over the chicken. Wash your hands.

6 Using oven gloves, put the roasting pan into the oven. Cook the chicken 8–10 minutes. Use oven gloves to remove the pan from the oven, chop open the biggest nugget with a clean knife to check it is cooked: The meat should be a solid white color (not at all translucent), with no traces of pink; if not put it back in the oven for a couple of minutes.

kebabs

Kebabs are small pieces of meat, usually beef or lamb, sometimes chicken, fish, or vegetables, threaded on to wooden or metal skewers and broiled, griddled, barbecued, or roasted. They were originally cooked in Turkey, became popular throughout the Middle East, and are now eaten all over the world. Anything cooked on a skewer like this can be called a kebab, even fruit! You can use either wooden or metal skewers, but if you use wooden skewers you will need to soak them in water for at least half an hour first to stop them from burning.

There are two main types of kebab: shish and doner. Shish kebabs are traditionally made from lamb or mutton, marinated (see below) in yogurt, oil, and spices, and cooked over hot embers or coals. Sometimes they are served on the skewers, and sometimes they are taken off on to a bed of rice, or couscous, or into pita bread. Doner kebabs are made from slices of meat threaded on to a large skewer or spit, which is turned constantly, over several hours, so that the meat cooks evenly. The meat is then sliced off in long thin pieces and served in pita bread with salad and yogurt.

The ingredients for kebabs need a firm texture so they do not fall apart during cooking. When preparing a kebab, you will need to cut all the pieces the same size so that they cook evenly.

marinades

It is a good idea to marinate the kebab ingredients before you broil them. A marinade is a liquid that is flavored with herbs or spices. It may contain oil, lemon juice, vinegar, wine, or yogurt. Food, usually meat, fish, or vegetables, is soaked in this liquid for an hour, overnight, or sometimes for longer. This process is called marinating. Its purpose is to give flavor to the food, but also to make it more tender and keep it moist during cooking. For example, try mixing 2 tablespoons of soy sauce with 2 tablespoons of runny honey, the juice of half a lemon, and a peeled and crushed garlic clove. This is perfect for chicken or pork. Or mix 1 tablespoon of lemon juice with 2 tablespoons of olive oil and a peeled and crushed garlic clove for a marinade for shrimp.

For fruit kebabs, such as banana and pineapple, try drizzling over honey or brushing with butter and then sifting over a little confectioners' sugar and broiling until the sugar starts to caramelize.

making the kebabs

If you are making a kebab that combines meat and vegetables, it is a good idea to alternate the ingredients. **Ⓐ** For example, to make the Thai chicken kebabs on page 33, thread a piece of chicken on to the skewer, then add a piece of bell pepper, then another piece of chicken, and so on until the skewer is full. **Ⓑ** Continue threading on to skewers in this way until you have no ingredients left.

cooking the kebabs

There are a few ways to cook kebabs: put the food under a hot broiler, on a barbecue, in a ribbed skillet, or in a hot oven. I prefer use a ribbed skillet, because the food cooks quickly and the direct contact with the hot skillet gives the food a lovely, slightly charred flavor, and helps to seal the juices inside the food.

kebabs

Marinating is a great technique, especially if you like cooking meat and fish. Marinades add a subtle flavor to the food, and adding lemon or lime juice will help to make the meat or fish really tender and juicy (see page 31). Satay sauce is made with peanuts, sometimes with added spices.

Thai chicken kebabs with satay sauce

SERVES 4

YOU WILL NEED:
INGREDIENTS
- juice of 1 lime
- 2 tsp Thai red curry paste
- ½ cup coconut milk
- 3 boneless skinless chicken breasts
- 1 red bell pepper

for the satay sauce:
- ¾ cup coconut milk
- ½ level tsp Thai red curry paste
- ⅔ cup crunchy peanut butter with no added salt
- 1 teaspoon brown sugar

EQUIPMENT
- small saucepan
- large shallow bowl
- small whisk
- 2 chopping boards
- 2 knives
- metal skewers or wooden kebab sticks, soaked in water for at least half an hour
- plastic wrap
- wooden spoon
- roasting pan
- oven gloves

1 Put 1 tablespoon of the lime juice into a small saucepan and put to one side for the peanut sauce. Put the red curry paste, coconut milk, and the rest of the lime juice into a large shallow bowl, then whisk together.

2 Put the chicken on a chopping board. Using a knife, cut the chicken into ½ inch cubes.

3 Put the bell pepper on a separate chopping board, cut in half, and remove the seeds. Cut it into the same sized pieces as the chicken.

4 Make the chicken kebabs (see page 31). Put all the kebabs into the bowl with the coconut milk marinade. Push them down and turn them over so they are covered in the mixture. Cover the bowl with plastic wrap and leave to marinate in the refrigerator at least an hour.

5 To make the satay sauce, pour the coconut milk into the small saucepan with the lime juice, and add the curry paste and peanut butter. Heat gently, stirring often with a wooden spoon until the sauce is smooth and hot—this will take about 5 minutes.

6 Turn the oven on to 350°F.

7 Take the kebabs out of the marinade and lay them in a roasting pan. Pour over half the remaining marinade. Using oven gloves, put the pan in the heated oven and cook 10–15 minutes until the kebabs are crispy and sticky and the chicken is cooked (see page 30, point 7). Using oven gloves, take the pan out of the oven. Reheat the satay sauce gently and serve with the kebabs.

using ground meat

Ground meat tends to be made from beef or lamb, although some recipes call for ground pork. Ground beef is usually made from the meat left on the carcass, mainly from the chuck and round, and sometimes the brisket. It is used in a variety of ways, including in hamburgers, Bolognese sauce, and chili con carne. Ground lamb is ideal for dishes such as moussaka and shepherd's pie. Ground pork tends to be made from the hind quarters and can be used in dishes such as meatballs. The ground meat that you find in the supermarkets can be very finely ground and, when it is cooked, all the juices run out of it and it becomes insipid. If you buy ground meat from a butcher, you can ask for it to be ground a little coarser.

hamburgers

MAKES 8 SMALL BURGERS

Ground beef for a burger should have some fat in it; this will make your burger lovely and juicy. Ground sirloin steak is delicious but expensive. Ground chuck or round steak is also good.

YOU WILL NEED:

INGREDIENTS
- 2 scallions
- 1 lb good quality ground beef
- a pinch of salt and freshly ground black pepper
- 1 small garlic clove, peeled
- 8 hamburger buns or rolls
- 8 crunchy lettuce leaves, such as iceberg, little gem, or romaine
- 1 large beef tomato, sliced
- ketchup and mayonnaise, to serve

EQUIPMENT
- chopping board
- knife
- large bowl and plate
- garlic press
- broiler pan
- kitchen tongs

1 On a chopping board, use a knife to chop the hairy root end and the very dark leaves off the scallions. Cut up the trimmed scallions as finely as you can. Put them into a large bowl.

2 Add the ground beef, salt, and pepper to the bowl. **A** Crush the garlic in the garlic press and add that too. Mix everything together with your hands.

3 Take a quarter of the mixture and divide it in two. **B** Use your hands to roll each bit into a ball, then pat it flat into a burger shape and put on to a plate. Repeat with the rest of the mixture so you have 8 hamburgers.

4 Turn the broiler on to high. Put the hamburgers on the rack in the broiler pan and cook about 6 minutes, then use the tongs to carefully turn them over and cook another 6 minutes. To check that the hamburgers are cooked all the way through, cut the biggest one in half—if it looks pink in the middle, put all of the burgers back under the flame for a few more minutes.

5 Cut the buns in half across the middle and put a piece of lettuce on the bottom and a slice of tomato on top of it. Put a hamburger on top, add a little ketchup or mayonnaise, and put the top half of the bun on top of that.

how stock is raised for food

Nearly all the food that we eat every day comes from farms. Farming means using land to rear animals and to grow crops to provide food for people to eat. Farming began when, instead of hunting animals, people started to gather wild goats and sheep into herds.

Long ago, these herds were moved from one place to another to find fresh areas for grazing. It was only when people started to grow crops for their own food and animals that real farming began. People stayed in one area and developed the land around them, relying on the crops and animals for food to feed themselves and their families. As they became more skillful at farming they could grow more than they needed. This surplus food could be exchanged for other foods, such as sugar, or cloth.

Gradually farming became more and more sophisticated, with a whole variety of machinery and tools introduced to make life easier and more efficient for farmers. In the last fifty or so years the use of chemicals in the form of pesticides and fertilizers, and the use of genetically modified crops (GM), has revolutionized farming.

The most extreme type of this is intensive farming, where hedges are destroyed and large areas of land are made into enormous fields. There is growing concern that this way of farming is not good for the environment or for us. In many parts of the world farmers are trying to return to old-fashioned methods of farming, where stock and crops are raised naturally and humanely, with respect for the world in which we live.

sheep
Sheep are kept for their wool, meat, and milk. Lamb is meat from young animals and mutton from slightly older animals. Mutton can actually be meat from any lamb over one year old. You will probably be most familiar with eating lamb stew, lamb chops and legs of lamb that are often roasted for special dinners.

cattle
Cattle can be kept for milk (dairy cows), which is sold for drinking or made into dairy products, such as cheese, yogurt, and butter. Alternatively they can be reared for meat (beef cattle). Although it is rare for cattle to be raised for both meat and milk, dairy cows can be sold for meat. A variety of different cuts of meat come from cows, including sirloin steak and filet mignon and shank, which is perfect for slow cooking to make stews and casseroles. Also some of the meat, mainly from the chuck and round, is ground (used in recipes like hamburgers).

pigs
Pigs are also kept for their meat. Some farms raise pigs indoors in big sheds, which are often just like battery hen farms (see page 49) but for pigs. Pigs raised outside are tough outdoor breeds, which produce very good meat. It is much nicer for pigs to be raised outdoors, where they can wallow in mud to cool down

and root with their snouts in the ground for things like acorns. Pigs are very sociable animals and like to be around other pigs. Some of the most popular foods from pigs are sausages, pork chops, and bacon.

chickens
Just like hens kept for their eggs, many chickens reared for meat are subjected to a poor quality of life. They can be crammed into sheds with artificial light, fed a high protein diet, and routinely given antibiotics. Free range chickens, however, are given the chance to roam around outside, nibbling at worms and scratching the ground. It is important to remember that the eating quality of any bird depends on three factors: the breed, a wholesome diet, and being allowed to roam outside. Roasting the whole bird is very popular, and it can be seasoned with butter and herbs to make it particularly tasty (see page 44). Chicken breasts are popular cuts of the bird, as are chicken thighs and drumsticks.

frying meat

There are two ways to fry meat. One way is to cook it so that you can eat it immediately—for example, frying a steak or lamb chop. The meat is fried over a medium or high heat, often with little or no oil because as the meat is cooked the fat it contains is released. This method of frying is often called "sautéing."

The second way to fry meat is to give flavor and color to a dish. The meat is fried quickly in oil, in a large heavy-based skillet over a high heat, until the outside is golden. The inside may not necessarily be cooked through, because the cooking will be finished later. For example, you may fry cubes of beef or lamb, and then finish the cooking in a stew or casserole. This method of frying is often called "browning."

spaghetti carbonara

SERVES 4

YOU WILL NEED:

INGREDIENTS
- 2 whole eggs
- 2 egg yolks
- 6 tablespoons heavy cream
- ¼ cup finely grated Parmesan
- a large pinch of coarse salt and freshly ground black pepper
- ½ lb bacon or cubes of pancetta (Italian bacon)
- 1 tbsp olive oil
- 1 lb spaghetti

EQUIPMENT
- small bowl
- fork
- kitchen scissors
- skillet
- long-handled wooden spoon
- large saucepan with lid
- oven gloves
- colander

1 Crack an egg into a small bowl by tapping the egg firmly against the side of the bowl, pushing your thumbs into the crack, and carefully pulling the shell apart, letting the egg drop into the bowl. Repeat with the second egg. Add the yolks, cream, cheese, and a pinch of salt and pepper and beat with a fork.

2 Using scissors, snip the bacon into small pieces. Heat the oil in a skillet, add the bacon, turn the heat up a little, and leave to cook 2 minutes.  Turn the bacon over carefully, stirring occasionally with the wooden spoon. Cook about 5 minutes. Remove the pan from the heat.

3 Three-quarters fill a large saucepan with water. Add a large pinch of salt, cover with a lid, and bring to a boil. Add the spaghetti, wait for it to soften, then use the long-handled wooden spoon to push it down into the water.

4 Bring back to a boil, turn down to a simmer, and cook according to the package instructions (see page 125, points 4–6). When the pasta is cooked, use oven gloves to bring the pan to the sink and drain the pasta in a colander (the pan may be heavy, so ask an adult for help with this). Tip the pasta back into the pan and add the bacon. Return the pan to the hob and cook over a low heat 1 minute, stirring well with the wooden spoon.

5 Pour over the egg mixture and stir constantly for 1 minute. Remove the pan from the heat and continue to stir for 2–3 minutes. The heat from the saucepan and pasta will cook the eggs. Serve immediately.

frying meat

"Hot dog" may seem like a funny name for a sausage in a bun, but when you look at its history it all makes sense. German immigrants to the U.S.A. started selling sausages in buns from street carts in New York as long ago as the 1860s. In Germany they were often called "little dogs", because they looked a little bit like dachshunds or "sausage dogs." The snack became more and more popular and Americans started to call them "hot dogs."

mini hot dogs

MAKES 4

YOU WILL NEED:
INGREDIENTS
- 1 red onion
- 2 tablespoons olive oil
- 4 good-quality frankfurters
- 1 medium French bread
- ketchup or mustard, to serve

EQUIPMENT
- 2 chopping boards
- knife
- skillet
- wooden spoon
- slotted spoon
- plate
- kitchen foil
- kitchen tongs
- fork
- breadboard
- bread knife

1 Put the onion on a chopping board and, using a knife, cut it in half. Peel the onion, then slice it as thinly as you can (see page 100).

2 Heat the oil in a skillet, add the onion, and cook 5 minutes, until soft, stirring with a wooden spoon. Using a slotted spoon, lift the onion on to a plate and cover with foil to keep it warm.

3 Put the skillet back over a medium heat. Add the frankfurters and fry for 7 minutes, turning often until they are golden brown all over. Take the skillet off the heat.

4 Using tongs, put the frankfurters on to a clean chopping board. Hold a frankfurter steady with a fork (they will be very hot) and, using a knife, cut the frankfurter in half lengthwise. Repeat with the other frankfurters.

5 Put the frankfurters, cut-side down, back in the skillet and cook them over a medium heat 1–2 more minutes, until cooked. Take the pan off the heat.

6 Using a breadboard and a bread knife, cut the French bread into 4 equal pieces a little shorter than a frankfurter. Carefully cut each piece in half lengthwise, but do not to cut all the way through the bread.

7 Open out each slice of French bread by pressing on it lightly. Put an equal amount of onion on the 4 pieces. Rest 2 halves of frankfurter in each one, letting a bit stick out on either side of the bread so that they look like long frankfurters. Top each one with a good squirt of ketchup or mustard.

broiling meat

Broiled meat is cooked quickly, and often gets a charred surface, which gives it a great flavor. To insure this happens, the broiler must be preheated to its highest setting—this may take around 10 minutes.

Because broiling does not make meat more tender, as stewing or slow-roasting does, only tender cuts of meat should be broiled. For example, sirloin steaks, hamburgers made from good quality ground meat, chicken breasts, and pork or lamb chops are all fine for broiling.

It is often good to marinate meat before broiling (see page 31), because this helps keep it moist under the high heat. Never add salt to meat before you broil it, because the salt will draw out the juices that you are trying to keep inside. Also, never overcook the meat or it may become dry.

simple lamb chops

SERVES 4

YOU WILL NEED:
INGREDIENTS
- 1 tablespoons olive oil
- 4 teaspoons mint jelly (optional)
- 4 lamb chops
- few rosemary sprigs

EQUIPMENT
- broiler pan
- kitchen foil and pastry brush
- small bowl
- oven gloves
- kitchen tongs and skewer

COOKING TIMES
Approx. times for broiling meat under a high heat:
- steak, 1 inch thick— approx. 1½-2 minutes each side for rare; 3 minutes each side for medium; 4 minutes each side for well done
- pork chops—approx. 10 minutes each side, depending on size
- loin lamb chops—approx. 10 minutes each side, depending on size
- rib lamb chops—approx. 5 minutes each side, depending on size

1 Turn the broiler on to its highest setting—it may take up to 10 minutes to get really hot. This is important, because you want to cook the outside of the meat as quickly as possible to keep the inside tender and juicy.

2 Line a broiler pan with kitchen foil and use a pastry brush to brush a little oil all over the foil.

3 If used, put the mint jelly into a small bowl. **A** Brush the chops with oil and put them on to the broiler pan. Brush the mint jelly, if using, over the lamb chops and scatter over a few rosemary sprigs.

4 **B** Using oven gloves, put the broiler pan under the heat, ideally so that the meat is about 2–3 inches away from the heat.

5 Broil 10 minutes, then use oven gloves to take the broiler pan out of the oven and turn the chops over using tongs. Cook another 10 minutes.

6 To test if the lamb is cooked, push a skewer into the thickest part of the meat to see if the juices are the right color. Pink juices indicate blood, which tells you that the meat is not cooked through. If you are broiling lamb or beef, you may like the meat to be slightly rare in the middle, but pork should always be cooked right through.

roasting meat

Oven roasting means cooking meat in the oven with a little fat—for example, drizzled with some olive oil or rubbed with butter. The great thing about roasting is that, although it takes a while, you don't have to do much while the meat is cooking. You may need to baste the meat (spoon the cooking juices over it to stop it from drying out) halfway through cooking.

The best meats to roast are the ones between tender and tough—for example, a leg of lamb, a whole chicken, a belly of pork or a rib of beef. Ideally you want meat on the bone, which will give it a very good flavor.

roast chicken

SERVES 4–6

There are two main ways of roasting a chicken: fast at a high temperature, or slow at a lower temperature. If you're cooking the bird slowly, it needs to be regularly basted. I prefer the quicker method because the chicken stays moist, and it is simple to do.

YOU WILL NEED:
INGREDIENTS
- ¼ stick softened butter, plus a small piece for greasing pan
- 2 tablespoons chopped fresh herbs, such as tarragon, rosemary, or parsley
- 1 chicken approx 3 lbs
- 1 onion, peeled
- a pinch each of salt and freshly ground black pepper
- 3 slices bacon

for the gravy:
- 1 tablespoon all-purpose flour
- 1 ¼ cups good chicken or vegetable stock or vegetable water

EQUIPMENT
- roasting pan
- small bowl
- metal spoon
- large plate
- knife
- chopping board
- oven gloves
- skewer
- 2 fish turners
- serving dish
- kitchen foil
- wooden spoon

1 Take the chicken out of the refrigerator about 30 minutes before you need to cook it. Turn the oven on to 450°F. Rub the base and sides of the roasting pan with a little butter.

2 Put the butter and the herbs into a small bowl and use your hand or a metal spoon to mix well. Put the chicken on a large plate and remove any string. Using clean hands, rub half of the herb butter inside the cavity of the chicken and the other half over the outside, using your fingers to push some of the butter under the skin of the breasts without tearing the skin.

3 Using a knife and a chopping board, cut the onion into 8 wedges and push these into the cavity of the chicken. Season with salt and pepper and place the bacon slices across the breast. Place in the roasting pan and, using oven gloves, put the pan in the oven. Roast 50 minutes then, using oven gloves, take the pan out of the oven.

4 There are two ways to check if the chicken is cooked. Push a skewer into the thickest part of the leg, take it out, and press it flat against the flesh to see if the juices run clear. Alternatively give the leg a tug—if it comes away from the body easily the chicken is cooked. You may need to cook the chicken another 10 minutes otherwise.

5 Using 2 fish turners, lift the chicken on to a warm serving dish. Cover with foil and leave to rest for 15 minutes, so the juices run back into the meat, keeping it all juicy and moist.

6 To make the gravy, slowly pour most of the fat out of the roasting pan, trying to keep as much of the juice as possible. Put the pan on to the hob and heat the fat over a medium heat. Add the flour and, using a wooden spoon, stir for 1 minute. Add the stock or vegetable water and stir until the sauce boils (3–4 minutes). Simmer 3 minutes. Add a pinch of salt and pepper.

3 FROM THE DAIRY

Eggs

Traditionally, most farms and many families kept hens. It was much more economical than buying eggs because hens are relatively easy to keep and can be fed with kitchen scraps, such as vegetable peelings and bacon rind.

In this way most people, even those without much space, were able to have lovely fresh eggs every day.

Hens reared in this old-fashioned way are allowed to roam outside all day, scratching in the dirt, looking for worms, grains, and bugs to eat. In case you were wondering, hens are not vegetarian!

Even on a big farm where hens can wander freely, they will not fly away or roam too far, they always stay near to their nests. When it starts to get dark the hens naturally head back to the henhouse where they roost for the night. The hen-house must be shut to keep the hens safe from predators such as foxes. First thing in the morning the door is opened so that the hens can come back out.

A healthy hen will lay between 180 and 320 eggs per year. The amount can vary between hens depending on their breed, age, diet, and even the time of year—hens tend to lay more in the summer. The hen will usually come out of the henhouse and cluck loudly after she has laid an egg.

Fewer people keep hens in this way today because eggs are so widely available in supermarkets and they are very cheap. But people are gradually beginning to realize that keeping hens can be fun and the eggs from your own hens often taste much better because of their varied diet. Hens reared at home, or on smaller chicken farms, often have a much nicer life than hens from enormous battery farms.

It can appear to be easy to keep hens and, once you are set up with two or three hens, a henhouse, and a big run, you will probably only need to spend 10 minutes a day feeding them and letting them into (and bringing them back in from) the yard. But if you are eager to keep hens, find out whether there are any reasons why you should not keep poultry in your area. Also, don't forget to speak to your neighbors.

battery farms

Of all eggs on sale today in the U.S.A. approximately 99 percent are laid by hens kept in battery cages.

Battery houses are big sheds, which often have no windows, so they have little natural light or fresh air. Each shed can hold 30,000–100,000 hens. To fit this number of hens into one shed each hen is kept in a little cage. When the hen lays an egg, it rolls down into a tray, where it is collected. All the hen cages are piled on top of each other—it is like a prison for hens.

barn eggs

Barn hens are kept in a similar way to battery hens, although they are allowed to roam all over the barn rather than being kept in a cage. However, barns can be just as crowded as a battery farm.

free range eggs

Free range hens can go outside, but their outside space is limited, although it does vary from farm to farm. They get some daylight and can peck and scratch the ground like they would naturally. Generally, the smaller free range egg producers look after their hens well.

organic eggs

Organic hens are usually kept in smaller flocks and generally they have more space. They also have easy access to outside areas where they can roam over organic land and they are fed organic feed.

We tend to use the word "chicken" to describe the meat we eat from a hen. A flock of the birds can be called hens or chickens, but a girl chicken is a hen and a boy chicken is a rooster (or a cockerel in the U.K.). Egg shells can be white or brown, but there is no difference in the taste. The shell's color is determined by the breed of hen that laid it. There are lots of breeds of chickens, some have amazing colored feathers and plumage, especially roosters.

boiling eggs

Boiling eggs is simple, so once you have mastered the art, boiled egg and toast makes a fun and easy meal. Be sure to use fresh free range eggs that are well within their "use by" date and avoid giving uncooked eggs to very small children.

boiled egg and soldiers

SERVES 1

YOU WILL NEED:

INGREDIENTS
- 1 medium egg
- 1 slice of bread
- a knob of butter

EQUIPMENT
- saucepan
- long-handled slotted spoon
- egg timer or watch
- eggcup
- spoon
- toaster
- chopping board
- knife

1 If your egg has been kept in the refrigerator, it will need to warm up before you boil it, so put it into a saucepan with cold water and bring to a boil.

2 If your egg has been kept out of the refrigerator, three-quarters fill a saucepan with water and bring to a boil. Lower your egg into the saucepan using a long-handled slotted spoon.

3 As soon as the water comes to a boil, set the timer for 4 minutes. This will give you a soft-boiled egg, with a runny yolk for dipping toast pieces into. If you prefer a hard-boiled egg with a firm yolk, set the timer for 7 minutes. If you are cooking a large egg, add 1 minute to the cooking time.

4 Ⓐ When your egg is done, lift it out of the pan with the slotted spoon. Ⓑ Put it into an eggcup and leave to cool slightly before you break the top off with a spoon.

5 Pop your bread into the toaster and cook until golden brown. Put it on to a chopping board and spread it with butter. Cut it into 4 long strips.

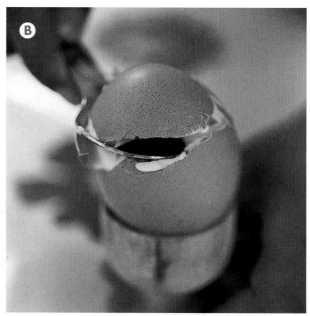

scrambling eggs

If you are making scrambled eggs for a special occasion, maybe for your mom on Mother's Day, add a little cream instead of milk. Scrambled eggs are good served on toast.

SERVES 4

YOU WILL NEED:

INGREDIENTS
- 8 medium eggs
- 6 tablespoons whole milk (or 3 tablespoons each of milk and light cream)
- a pinch of salt and freshly ground black pepper
- a big knob of butter

EQUIPMENT
- medium bowl
- fork
- medium skillet

1 Crack an egg into a medium bowl by tapping the egg firmly against the side of the bowl, pushing your thumbs into the crack, and carefully pulling the shell apart, letting the egg drop into the bowl. Repeat with the remaining eggs.

2 Add the milk and/or cream and salt and pepper. **A** Beat with a fork.

3 Melt the butter in a medium skillet over a medium heat. Gently tip the pan so that the sides are coated with butter.

4 When the butter just begins to bubble, pour in the beaten eggs.

5 **B** Stir gently with a wooden spoon, moving the mixture all around the skillet to prevent the eggs from sticking to the bottom. When all the runny bits of egg have been cooked—this will take 3–4 minutes—take the skillet off the heat. Serve immediately.

poaching eggs

When poaching eggs, it is important to use the freshest eggs you can, under four days old if possible, because they will hold their shape well. Adding a little vinegar to the water will also help the eggs hold their shape—but don't worry, you can't taste it! Avoid giving uncooked eggs to very small children.

SERVES 2

YOU WILL NEED:
INGREDIENTS
- 1 teaspoon vinegar
- 2 eggs

EQUIPMENT
- medium to large skillet
- small pitcher
- small bowl
- egg timer or watch
- kitchen paper
- plate
- slotted spoon

GOOD THINGS TO EAT WITH POACHED EGGS
✔ baked beans
✔ grilled bacon
✔ salad (see page 109)
✔ grilled mushrooms
✔ big chips (see page 92)

1 Put a skillet on the hob, then use a pitcher to fill it three-quarters full with cold water. Add the vinegar and stir.

2 On a low heat, bring the water just to simmering point. You should be able to see tiny bubbles simmering on the bottom of the pan, but not on the surface of the water.

3 Ⓐ Crack an egg into a small bowl by tapping the egg firmly against the side of the bowl, pushing your thumbs into the crack, and carefully pulling the shell apart, letting the egg drop into the bowl. Ⓑ Carefully tip the egg into the pan. Repeat with the remaining egg and add it to the skillet, making sure the eggs are not touching.

4 Set the egg timer for 1 minute, but watch the skillet to make sure it doesn't boil. The gently simmering water will set the outside of the egg white, which will prevent the egg from spreading; if it boils, the egg white can separate into thin ribbons.

5 Turn the heat off and move the skillet to the cool side of the hob. Set the egg timer for 10 minutes—the eggs will continue to cook in the hot water even though the skillet is off the heat.

6 Put 2–3 sheets of paper towels on to a plate. Put the skillet next to the plate. Use a slotted spoon to lift an egg on to the paper towels to drain. Repeat with the other egg. Serve immediately.

poaching eggs

This salad has a lovely combination of textures: soft eggs, crunchy croûtons, and crisp lettuce. It makes a great summery lunch. Be sure to use fresh free range eggs that are well within their "use by" date and avoid giving uncooked eggs to very small children.

warm poached egg and bacon salad

SERVES 4

YOU WILL NEED:
INGREDIENTS
- 2 thick slices of white bread
- 6 tablespoons olive oil
- 8 bacon slices
- 1 teaspoon vinegar
- 4 medium eggs
- 1 medium romaine lettuce, washed
- 2 tablespoons lemon juice
- 1 teaspoon balsamic vinegar
- a pinch of soft brown sugar
- a pinch of salt and freshly ground black pepper

EQUIPMENT
- chopping board
- knife
- 3 small bowls
- 2 medium baking trays
- oven gloves
- kitchen scissors
- 5 plates
- medium to large skillet
- slotted spoon
- kitchen paper
- whisk

1 Turn the oven on to 400°F. Put the bread on to a chopping board and, using a knife, cut each slice into strips, then cut each strip into small cubes.

2 For the croûtons, put the bread cubes into a bowl, add 2 tablespoons of the oil and use your hands to mix them around until they are covered in oil.

3 Put the bread cubes on to a baking sheet and spread them out evenly. Put the bacon on to a second baking sheet.

4 Using oven gloves, put the bacon into the oven on the top shelf and cook for 6 minutes. Put the bread into the oven alongside the bacon and cook for 6–8 minutes.

5 Using oven gloves, take the baking sheets out of the oven. Use scissors to snip the bacon into small pieces and put into a small bowl.

6 Poach the eggs (see page 53).

7 Tear the lettuce leaves into small pieces and divide among 4 plates. Sprinkle over the bacon and croûtons. Put an egg on top of each plate.

8 Put the remaining oil, lemon juice, balsamic vinegar, sugar, and salt and pepper into a bowl. Beat together and then drizzle over the salads. Serve immediately.

omelets

Omelets are a little challenging, if only because you have to try and get them out of the skillet in one piece! But once you've mastered them, there are lots of fillings you can add.

cheese omelet

SERVES 1

YOU WILL NEED:
INGREDIENTS
- ⅓ cup Cheddar or Swiss cheese, grated
- 2 medium eggs
- a pinch of salt and freshly ground black pepper
- 1 tablespoon cold water
- a knob of butter
- 1 teaspoon olive oil

EQUIPMENT
- cheese grater
- small plate and medium bowl
- fork
- skillet
- wooden spoon
- palette knife

GOOD THINGS TO SPRINKLE OVER YOUR OMELET
- ✔ different types of grated cheese, such as Red Leicester
- ✔ crumbled blue cheese
- ✔ chopped cooked ham
- ✔ crumbled cooked bacon
- ✔ fried sliced mushrooms
- ✔ a little chopped parsley or tarragon

1 Coarsely grate the cheese on to a plate (see page 69).

2 Crack an egg into a medium bowl by tapping the egg firmly against the side of the bowl, pushing your thumbs into the crack, and carefully pulling the shell apart, letting the egg drop into the bowl. Do the same with the second egg. Add the salt and pepper and then the water— this makes the omelet lighter.

3 Use a fork to gently mix the eggs: Don't beat them, just mix the yolk and white together.

4 Melt the butter and oil together in a skillet over a medium heat.

5 **(A)** Turn up the heat and, as soon as the butter starts to foam, pour in the beaten eggs. Quickly tilt the skillet so that the egg mixture covers the base evenly.

6 **(B)** Count to ten, then use a wooden spoon to pull the set egg from the sides of the pan, towards the middle. Doing this allows the runny egg to move to the edge of the pan, so that the omelet cooks evenly. This will take about a minute.

7 When the bottom is cooked but there is still some runny egg on top, sprinkle over the grated cheese.

8 Slide the palette knife under one side of the omelet and quickly fold it over. Quickly tilt the pan so the omelet slides, still folded, on to your plate.

batter

The batters for toad in the hole, Yorkshire puddings, pancakes, and drop biscuits are all made in a similar way, but the quantities of ingredients may vary.

toad in the hole

SERVES 4

Don't open the oven while these toads are cooking, because the cold air will make the batter collapse.

YOU WILL NEED:
INGREDIENTS
- 1 ¼ cups all-purpose flour
- a pinch of coarse salt and freshly ground black pepper
- ½ cup milk
- ½ cup water
- 2 large eggs
- 6 teaspoons vegetable oil
- 12 tiny good quality cocktail sausages

EQUIPMENT
- flour sifter
- large bowl
- 2 pitchers
- small bowl
- fork
- wooden spoon
- whisk
- 12-hole muffin pan
- oven gloves
- kitchen tongs
- palette knife

1 Turn the oven on to 425°F.

2 To make the batter (see page 62), sift the flour into a large bowl, then add the salt and pepper. Make a well in the middle of the flour.

3 Mix the milk and water together in a pitcher. Crack the eggs into a small bowl and beat together lightly with a fork.

4 Pour the eggs into the well in the flour. Use a wooden spoon to gradually stir the eggs into the flour. As the mixture thickens, pour in the milk and water a little at a time, and gently mix until you have a smooth batter. Pour the batter into a clean pitcher.

5 Put ½ teaspoon of oil into each hole in a muffin pan. Using oven gloves, put the pan into the oven 5 minutes. Using oven gloves, take the pan out of the oven and put on to a pan stand—the oil will be really hot so be careful; you may need to get an adult to help.

6 Using kitchen tongs, put a cocktail sausage into each hole in the pan. Using oven gloves, put the pan back into the oven 15 minutes until the sausages are golden brown. Using oven gloves, take the pan out of the oven and rest on a pan stand. Pour the batter into the muffin holes.

7 Using oven gloves, put the pan straight into the oven 12–14 minutes until the batter has puffed up and is golden brown and crispy.

8 Using oven gloves, remove the pan from the oven. Leave to cool in the pan for 1 minute before using a palette knife to remove each toad from the pan. Serve immediately.

batter

blueberry pancakes

SERVES 4

Blueberry pancakes are usually eaten for breakfast, often drizzled with warm maple syrup.

YOU WILL NEED:
INGREDIENTS
- ¼ lb apples
- 1 tablespoon unsalted butter, plus a little knob for frying
- 1 large egg
- 1 ¼ cups buttermilk
- 2 drops vanilla extract
- 1 ¼ cups all-purpose flour
- 1 teaspoon bicarbonate of soda
- ½ teaspoon cinnamon
- 1 ¼ fresh blueberries
- 1 teaspoon vegetable oil
- 4 tablespoons maple syrup or honey, to serve

EQUIPMENT
- vegetable peeler
- knife
- 2 small saucepans
- 2 large bowls
- whisk
- flour sifter
- wooden spoon
- skillet
- spoon
- palette knife
- plate
- kitchen foil
- small pitcher

1 Peel, core and chop the apples into pieces the same size as the blueberries.

2 Put the tablespoon of butter into a small saucepan and melt over a medium heat. Remove from the heat and allow to cool slightly.

3 Put the egg, buttermilk, vanilla, and melted butter into a large bowl and whisk. Sift the flour, bicarbonate of soda, and cinnamon into another large bowl and make a well in the center.

4 Pour the egg mixture into the well and use a wooden spoon to stir the liquid to make a whirlpool in the middle of the bowl. This will gradually pull the flour into the liquid—don't stir the flour, just keep stirring the liquid. Don't over mix the batter; lumps are fine. When it is well combined, stir in the apples and blueberries.

5 Heat the oil and knob of butter in a skillet until the butter just starts to bubble.

6 Drop spoonfuls of batter into the pan, spaced well apart so they don't stick together. Cook for 2 minutes, until bubbles start to rise on the surface. Slide a palette knife under each pancake and quickly flip it over.

7 Cook for another 2 minutes, then lift the pancakes out on to a plate using the palette knife. Cover the plate with foil to keep the pancakes warm. Cook the remaining batter in the same way.

8 Put the maple syrup or honey into a small saucepan and warm very gently over a medium heat. Pour the syrup into a jug and serve it drizzled over the warm pancakes.

batter

pancakes

MAKES 12 PANCAKES

These pancakes taste delicious with fresh fruit, lemon and sugar, or even jam.

YOU WILL NEED:

INGREDIENTS

- 1 cup all-purpose flour
- a pinch of salt
- 2 large eggs
- 1 cup milk
- ½ cup water
- ¼ stick butter, melted, plus a little extra for frying
- 1 tablespoons vegetable oil

EQUIPMENT

- flour sifter and small pitcher
- 1 large and 1 small bowl
- fork
- small wooden spoon and hand whisk
- spatula and dish towel
- skillet, palette knife, and plate
- kitchen foil

GOOD THINGS TO EAT WITH PANCAKES

- ✔ freshly squeezed lemon juice and caster sugar
- ✔ strawberry jam
- ✔ sliced bananas and soft brown sugar
- ✔ chocolate spread

1 Sift the flour and salt into a large bowl, holding the sifter high above the bowl. Tap an egg firmly against the side of a small bowl, push your thumbs into the crack, and carefully pull the shell apart, letting the egg drop into the bowl. Repeat with the second egg. Beat the eggs with a fork until the whites and yolks are mixed.

2 Mix the milk and water together in a small pitcher. Make a well in the center of the flour. Pour in the beaten eggs and 2 tablespoons of the milk mixture. **A** Using a small wooden spoon, stir the eggs and milk to make a whirlpool in the middle of the bowl. This will gradually pull the flour into the liquid. Don't stir in the flour—just keep stirring the liquid. When the liquid is as thick as heavy cream, pour in a little more milk mixture and continue to mix, pulling in more flour.

3 Continue, alternately mixing and adding liquid, until all the milk is used up. Run a spatula around the bowl to dislodge any bits of flour and beat the mixture so you have a smooth, lump free batter. **B** Using a whisk, beat in the melted butter. Leave the batter to stand, covered with a dish towel, at least 30 minutes.

4 Put 1 teaspoon of oil and a little butter in a skillet over a medium heat. When hot, pour 3 tablespoons of batter into the skillet. Swirl the mixture around the skillet so that the base is covered, then pour any excess mixture back into the bowl.

5 Cook the pancake for a minute or so, then use a palette knife to flip it over. Cook for another minute or so, then tip it out on to a plate. Cover with foil to keep warm. Keep making pancakes until all the batter is used up—you may need to add more oil and butter to the pan after 6 pancakes.

whisking

You whisk things to add air to them, which makes dishes lighter and fluffier. There are a few types of whisks: a big food mixer with an egg beater attachment, a hand electric mixer, or a simple hand whisk or eggbeater. All of these work fine, but some are quicker than others. Many dishes, such as meringue or chocolate mousse, look and taste fantastic because some of the ingredients are whisked. As well as making a dish lighter, air bubbles act as a rising agent—they heat up in the oven and get bigger, making dishes, such as cakes or soufflés, even lighter. Stiff peaks occur when the egg foam holds its shape firmly and no longer wobbles on the tip of the whisk or beater. Ideally the foam should not be too dry; it should still look slightly moist. Try not to over beat the foam because it can then collapse.

YOU WILL NEED:

INGREDIENTS
- eggs

EQUIPMENT
- 1 large bowl and 2 small bowls
- teaspoon and dish towel
- hand whisk (optional) and electric mixer

WHAT TO USE WHISKING FOR
- ✔ fruit fools
- ✔ mousses
- ✔ soufflés
- ✔ whisked cakes
- ✔ soufflé omelets that puff up in the pan

1 Ⓐ Tap your first egg firmly against the side of a large, clean, dry bowl, push your thumbs into the crack, and carefully pull the shell apart, keeping the yolk in one half of the shell. Tip the yolk from one half of the shell to the other, letting the white dribble into the bowl. Put the yolk in a small bowl.

2 Break the second egg over a second small bowl. Tip the white into the big bowl and put the yolks together. Continue like this until you have as many egg whites as you need.

3 Check the whites for any bits of yolk or shell and remove with a teaspoon or empty shell half.

4 Rest the bowl of egg whites on a dish towel so it doesn't slip around. Ⓑ The first time you use a whisk, use a hand whisk to get a feel for whisking, but then swap to an electric mixer. Put the beaters in the bowl and begin at a low speed. Gradually increase the speed, moving the beaters in a figure-of-eight movement until the whites increase in volume and turn from clear to white.

5 Keep beating until stiff peaks form: If you tip the bowl gently, the peaks of the whites should slightly tip over. The egg whites are now ready to have sugar beaten in or to be folded into another mixture as they are into an omelet or soufflé.

whisking

toffee meringues with honeycomb cream

MAKES APPROX 30 LARGE OR 40 TINY MERINGUES

Who'd believe that something so yummy could be made out of egg whites? In the summer, when berries are in season, such as raspberries and strawberries, try adding a handful to some whipped cream and use to sandwich your meringues together.

YOU WILL NEED:
INGREDIENTS
- 3 medium egg whites
- ½ cup superfine sugar
- ⅓ cup light brown sugar
- 1 ¼ cups heavy cream
- 2 Crunchie bars (honeycomb coated in chocolate), or Clark bars, or home-made honeycomb (see page 174)

EQUIPMENT
- 2 baking sheets
- baking parchment
- 3 large bowls
- electric mixer
- tablespoon
- oven gloves
- plate
- plastic sandwich bag
- rolling pin
- metal spoon

1 Turn the oven on to 225°F. Line 2 baking sheets with baking parchment.

2 Separate the eggs (see page 63, point 1). Put the egg whites into a large bowl and beat until stiff peaks form (see page 63, points 4 and 5).

3 In a second large bowl, combine the two sugars. Beat 1 tablespoon of sugar into the egg whites. Add more sugar a spoonful at a time, whisking well after each spoonful, until half of the sugar is used up. Beat in the remaining half all at once until the mixture is thick and glossy.

4 Dot a little meringue mixture under the corners of the baking paper to help stick it to the baking sheets. Use a tablespoon to put blobs of the mixture on the lined sheets, leaving space between them. Wearing oven gloves, put the baking sheets in the oven. Cook for 1 hour.

5 Use oven gloves to take the meringues out of the oven. The middle of the meringues will be slightly squashy. When the meringues are cool, gently lift them off the paper and rest on a plate.

6 Put the cream in a clean large bowl and beat it until soft peaks form. Put the candy bars into a plastic bag and hit it with a rolling pin to make small pieces. Add the broken pieces to the whipped cream and, using a metal spoon, mix gently.

7 Spoon 1 tablespoon of the candy bar mixture on to the flat side of one of the meringues and sandwich another meringue on top. Repeat with the rest of the meringues and cream.

whisking

chocolate mousse

MAKES 4 LITTLE POTS OF MOUSSE

This is really rich, so make sure that you serve it in "small" cups or bowls. Use fresh free range eggs that are well within their "use by" date and avoid giving uncooked eggs to very small children.

YOU WILL NEED:

INGREDIENTS
- 6 oz good quality bittersweet chocolate
- 4 medium eggs, at room temperature
- ⅓ cup confectioners' sugar
- ¾ cup heavy cream

EQUIPMENT
- medium bowl
- medium saucepan
- 3 large bowls
- electric mixer or whisk
- flour sifter
- wooden spoon
- large metal spoon
- spatula
- 4 small ramekins

1 Melt the chocolate in a medium bowl over a pan of simmering water. Leave the chocolate to cool slightly.

2 Separate the eggs (see page 63, point 1).

3 Beat the egg whites to stiff peaks (see page 63, points 4 and 5). Sift the confectioners' sugar over the egg whites and beat again until it is mixed in.

4 Wash and dry the beaters or whisk. Then, in another large bowl, beat the cream until soft peaks form.

5 Beat the egg yolks lightly with a wooden spoon, then add the cooled melted chocolate and gently mix.

6 **A** Using a large metal spoon, fold 1 tablespoon of the whipped cream into the chocolate to loosen it. Fold in the rest of the cream, using a spatula to scrape it out of the bowl.

7 Use the metal spoon to fold 1 tablespoon of the whisked egg white into the chocolate mixture. Fold in the remaining egg white, carefully folding and cutting so that you keep as much air in the mousse as possible. Air is what gives the mousse its light texture.

8 **B** Spoon the mousse into the ramekins and leave to chill in the refrigerator for half an hour before serving.

FROM THE DAIRY 67

whisking

You can make fools from any kind of fruit, but it must be ripe. Soft fruits, such as raspberries, bananas, and strawberries, don't need to be cooked. Other fruit, such as apples, rhubarb, and gooseberries, just needs stewing, cooling, then puréeing. Fruit fool is good served with thin crisp cookies.

Caribbean mango fool

SERVES 4

YOU WILL NEED:

INGREDIENTS
- 1 large ripe mango (approx. ¾ lb flesh)
- 2 teaspoons lime juice
- 1 tablespoon light brown sugar
- 1 ¼ cup heavy cream
- 1 ¾ cups natural yogurt

EQUIPMENT
- chopping board
- knife
- 2 metal spoons
- pitcher
- hand blender, food processor. or blender
- large bowl
- whisk or electric mixed
- 4 glass serving dishes

1 Put the mango on to a chopping board and, using a knife, cut down either side of the pit. Use a metal spoon to scoop out the flesh, then put it into a pitcher. Cut any flesh from around the pit and add the flesh to the pitcher. Blend with a hand, blender (or in a food processor or blender) until smooth.

2 Stir in the lime juice and sugar (if the mango is really sweet and ripe, it may not need sugar).

3 Pour the cream into a large bowl and beat until it forms soft peaks.

4 Using a metal spoon, gently fold the yogurt into the cream, keeping as much air in the cream as possible because this is what will make the fool light.

5 (A) Pour over the mango purée and fold it in with a metal spoon. Don't worry about getting an even color.

6 Spoon the fool into 4 serving dishes. Serve immediately.

grating

The most common kind of grater is an upright metal four-sided grater with a handle on top so you can hold it steady. Stand it on a chopping board to stop it sliding around and choose the side you need to grate on. For example, if you are grating carrot for a salad, choose the side with the biggest holes. Ⓐ Hold the carrot firmly and rub it up and down on the grater. When you get near the end, tuck your fingers in and grate more carefully, or you will grate the ends of your fingers.

If you are grating a lot of something, it may be easier to use the grater attachment of a food processor. Get an adult to help you the first time you do this. There are several smaller graters, which are often used for grating things finely so that they can be sprinkled over food or into a dish. For example, there's a microplane grater for ginger, a nutmeg grater for hard whole nutmeg, or a lemon zester for taking just the zest and not the bitter pith from citrus fruit.

cheese
Grated cheese is delicious in a sandwich or on top of a pizza. It is often put into sauces because the grated pieces melt more quickly than a big lump. Cold cheese from the refrigerator is easier to grate than warm cheese. Hard cheese, such as Parmesan or Cheddar, is delicious grated and sprinkled over pasta, pizza, baked potatoes, or mashed potato topped pies.

carrots
Coarsely grated carrots are delicious in a salad, especially with raisins and toasted nuts or sunflower seeds. Grated carrot is also delicious fried—just melt a big knob of butter in a pan, add the carrot and cook over a gentle heat until the carrot is just tender. If you are using new season carrots, just scrub them well before grating; if you are using old carrots, peel them first.

zucchini
Coarsely grated zucchini are good gently fried in butter, especially with a little rosemary and a tablespoon of cream, then served with pasta.

chocolate
Ⓑ Grated chocolate looks lovely sprinkled over desserts, such as layer cakes, sundaes, hot chocolate or ice cream. Put the the chocolate in the refrigerator before you grate it or else it will quickly start to melt as you hold it Wrap the end you are holding in a little parchment paper to stop your fingers getting sticky.

apple or pear
Grated apple or pear (either peeled or unpeeled but washed) is delicious mixed into yogurt for breakfast or mixed with muesli. Grated apple is also good in salads, especially with grated carrot.

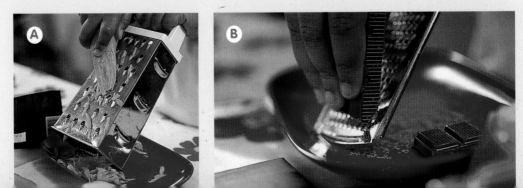

grating

classic cheese straws

MAKES 12 STRAWS

Preparing cheese straws is a great way to practice both grating and pastry making. The less you handle the ingredients, the lighter and crisper your straws will be. It is easier to grate the cheese when it's cold. If you're not a fan of Cheddar, use any other hard cheese, such as Swiss or Parmesan.

YOU WILL NEED:
INGREDIENTS
- ½ stick butter, chilled and cubed, plus extra for greasing
- ¾ cup all-purpose flour, plus extra for dusting
- a pinch of salt and freshly ground black pepper
- ⅓ cup grated strong Cheddar, (see page 69)
- 1 large egg, beaten with a fork

EQUIPMENT
- cheese grater
- baking sheet
- flour sifter
- large bowl
- metal spoon
- table knife
- rolling pin
- knife
- pastry brush
- oven gloves
- palette knife
- wire rack

1 Turn the oven on to 350°F. Rub a little butter all over a baking sheet.

2 Sift the flour into a large bowl and add the salt and pepper.

3 Using a metal spoon, stir the butter into the flour. Use your fingertips to rub it in until it looks like fine breadcrumbs (see page 88, points 3–4).

4 Using a metal spoon, stir the cheese into the flour and butter. Make a well in the center. Tip half of the beaten egg into the well. Using a table knife, stir the egg into the flour until the mixture starts to come together then, using your hand, work it into a ball.

5 Sprinkle flour on to the work surface and turn out the dough. Roll it into a ball, then pat it down so the surface is flat. Sprinkle flour over a rolling pin and roll out the dough to ⅕ inch thick.

6 Dip the blade of a knife in flour and use it to cut the pastry in half. Cut each piece into long thin straws. Lift them on to the baking sheet, leaving a little space between them. Use the pastry brush to brush some of the remaining beaten egg on to each straw.

7 Using oven gloves, put the baking sheet into the oven. Cook 10 minutes until golden.

8 Using oven gloves, take the tray out of the oven. Leave the straws to cool for a moment then, still with one oven glove on to hold the tray, use a palette knife to transfer them to a wire rack. Store in an airtight container.

grating

quick cheese twisties

MAKES 30 TWISTIES

These are quick to make and delicious. If you want to make sweet pastry twists, just replace the cheese and anchovy paste with jam or chocolate spread.

YOU WILL NEED:

INGREDIENTS
- a little butter, for greasing
- a little flour, for dusting
- 1 package of frozen puff pastry
- ¾ cup grated Cheddar cheese
- 1 level tablespoon anchovy paste

EQUIPMENT
- cheese grater and 2 baking sheets
- rolling pin
- knife and palette knife
- oven gloves and wire rack

OTHER THINGS TO MAKE TWISTIES WITH

Instead of anchovy paste you could use:
- ✔ ketchup
- ✔ tapenade
- ✔ 2 teaspoons of grainy mustard

1 Make sure that the puff pastry has thawed. Turn the oven on to 400°F. Rub a little butter all over 2 baking sheets.

2 Sprinkle the work surface with a little flour, then roll out the pastry according to the package instructions.

3 Sprinkle the cheese evenly over half the pastry, then fold the other half over the top of the cheese and press down. Using a rolling pin, roll the pastry out to its original size.

4 Using a palette knife, spread the anchovy paste evenly over half the pastry, then fold the other half on top of the anchovy paste and press down. Using a rolling pin, roll the pastry out to its original size.

5 Using a knife, cut the pastry into long thin straws. Hold the end of a straw in one hand and use your other hand to twist the other end. Lay it on the baking sheets. Repeat with the other straws, leaving a little space between them.

6 Using oven gloves, put the baking sheets into the oven and cook 8–10 minutes.

7 Using oven gloves, take the sheets out of the oven. Lift the straws off the tray and put them on to a wire rack.

using a sugar thermometer

vanilla fudge
MAKES 50 SMALL SQUARES

Homemade fudge makes a great present. Get an adult to help, especially with the beating and pouring, because the mixture will be really hot. When cooking the fudge, have your oven gloves and dish towel for resting the pan on ready, so you can remove the pan from the heat as soon as the sugar thermometer registers the right temperature.

YOU WILL NEED:

INGREDIENTS
- ¾ stick butter, plus extra for greasing
- 1 lb granulated sugar
- ⅔ cup whole milk
- ⅔ cup evaporated milk
- 2–3 drops vanilla extract

EQUIPMENT
- 8 inch square baking pan
- large heavy-based saucepan
- long-handled wooden spoon
- sugar thermometer
- oven gloves
- dish towel
- palette knife
- knife

GOOD THINGS TO ADD TO FUDGE
- ✔ chopped nuts, such as toasted almonds, walnuts
- ✔ dried fruit, such as raisins, cranberries, or chopped apricots
- ✔ for chocolate fudge, add 3 tablespoons of sifted cocoa

1 Rub a little butter all over the baking pan.

2 Put the sugar, butter, milk, and evaporated milk into a large heavy-based saucepan and heat gently on the hob, stirring often with a wooden spoon, until the sugar has dissolved. When it has dissolved, the base of the pan will feel smooth rather than grainy under the spoon.

3 Turn the heat up and bring the mixture to a boil, then turn the heat down slightly, keeping the mixture at a gentle boil. Rest a sugar thermometer in the pan and continue to boil, stirring occasionally, until the temperature reaches 240°F— this will take about 10 minutes (see page 76).

4 Using oven gloves, remove the pan from the heat immediately and rest it on a folded dish towel. Stir in the vanilla extract.

5 Let the mixture cool 1–2 minutes, then beat with a wooden spoon until it just starts to get thick and grainy and loses its shine— be careful because it will still be very hot.

6 Using oven gloves, carefully pour the fudge into the pan and use a palette knife to smooth the top. Using a knife, score the fudge into squares and leave to cool. Cut into squares and store in an airtight container.

using a sugar thermometer

A sugar thermometer is used to test the temperature of sugar during cooking. It is helpful when making sweet things, such as fudge, jam, caramel, or honeycomb. However, it is also useful for deep-frying things like fish or french fries, because you can measure the temperature of hot fat with it and prevent it from becoming overheated, which would be dangerous.

When sugar is cooked, the changing temperature has different effects on it. If it is melted and cooked a little, you can make syrup. If it is cooked more, you get a thicker syrup which, when cooled, will set thickly so that it can be spread like jam. If it is cooked for even longer and to a higher temperature, it will be firmer when it cools so that you can cut it into squares, as happens with toffee or fudge. If you keep cooking it, it will set so that when it is cold you can snap it, as happens with caramel or honeycomb.

Since the temperature of sugar can change quickly and it is hard to tell by eye how hot it is, having a sugar thermometer will help you get it right.

tips for using a sugar thermometer:

1 Your sugar thermometer must be clean and dry. Any bits of old sugar can make the mixture you are cooking crystallize, so instead of having a clear smooth mixture you will have a cloudy grainy mass. To clean the thermometer after use, soak it in a glass filled with very hot water.

2 Have everything ready before you put the sugar on the heat. The temperature of sugar can change quickly, so when it's ready you will need to take it off the heat as quickly and carefully as possible, asking an adult to help you. It can also start to set quickly once off the heat, so you need to pour the mixture into jars or tins straight away.

3 Read the recipe first and make sure you know where on the thermometer the heat marker needs to get to. The thermometer should be marked with degrees in centigrade (°C) and Fahrenheit (°F).

4 Use a pan with a thick, heavy base, because this will distribute heat better, cook the sugar more evenly, and give a more accurate reading on the thermometer.

5 Make sure the bottom of the thermometer is covered by about 1⅕ inches of liquid or else it won't read the heat accurately. Some sugar thermometers have a clip to attach them to the side of the pan so that you can stir and check the temperature at the same time.

6 Most sugar thermometers have a specially made handle that will not get hot during cooking, but it is still a good idea to lift the thermometer out using an oven glove because hot sugar often bubbles and spits and can burn you badly.

7 Watch the red line carefully—as soon as the mixture reaches the right temperature, use oven gloves to take the pan off the heat immediately – remember to get an adult to help you move the pan carefully.

custard and ice cream

You can flavor custard with lots of things, such as chocolate. Vanilla beans are among the favorite flavorings, and they come from a climbing orchid, usually from a country called Madagascar. A vanilla bean will give your custard and ice cream an intense but subtle vanilla flavor, especially if you leave the ice cream in the freezer for at least 24 hours to allow the flavor to develop.

custard-based vanilla ice cream

SERVES 6

If you don't have a vanilla bean use vanilla extract for this recipe instead, but avoid vanilla essence (which is an artificial flavoring).

YOU WILL NEED:

INGREDIENTS
- 1 ¼ cups whole milk
- 1 vanilla pod, split in half lengthways
- 3 egg yolks
- ½ cup superfine sugar
- 1 ¼ whipping cream

EQUIPMENT
- medium saucepan
- dish towel
- 2 medium bowls
- hand electric mixer
- spatula
- strainer
- wooden spoon
- knife
- large metal spoon
- freezer-proof container with a lid

1 For the custard, pour the milk into a medium saucepan, add the vanilla bean, and heat gently until tiny bubbles begin to form around the edge of the pan. Take the pan off the heat immediately. Leave 10 minutes to absorb the vanilla flavor (this is called infusing).

2 Fold a dish towel in half and place it under a medium bowl. Put the egg yolks into the bowl and add the sugar. Beat until the mixture is pale and thick enough to leave a ribbon shape on the top when the beaters are lifted.

3 Remove the vanilla bean from the milk and put it to one side. Continue to beat the egg mixture, using the lowest speed possible. Pour the milk into the egg mixture in a thin stream, beating all the time.

4 Rinse the saucepan, then pour in the custard, scraping the bowl out with a spatula. Let the cold water run a little, then pour a few inches of water into the sink. Place a strainer over a bowl next to the hob. Put the pan back on the hob over a very low heat. Stir the custard constantly with a wooden spoon, until it is thick enough to coat the back of the spoon (this may take 10–15 minutes). Do not turn up the heat or the custard will curdle (when the egg cooks too quickly and scrambles before it thickens the milk).

5 As soon as the custard is ready, take it off the heat and pour it through the strainer into the bowl. Put the bowl in the sink to help cool the custard. Using a knife, scrape the seeds out of the vanilla bean and stir them into the custard. For the ice cream, wait until the custard is cool, then put it into the refrigerator for at least an hour.

6 Wash and dry the beaters. Pour the cream into a bowl and beat until soft peaks form. Using a large metal spoon, fold in the cream. Pour into a freezer-proof container. Put the lid on and freeze at least 4 hours until it starts to freeze all around the edges.

7 Take the ice cream out of the container and put it in a food processor and process until smooth to remove the ice crystals and make the icecream easier to scoop. Pour it back in the container and freeze at least 6 hours. Take the ice cream out of the freezer 5 minutes before you want to eat it.

custard and ice cream

classic strawberry ice cream

SERVES 6–8

Making ice cream at home is much easier than you think. It takes a little bit of forward-planning, because, unless you have an ice-cream machine, you need to make it the day before you want to serve it. Once you have learned how to make this one, you can make lots of other flavors simply by changing the kind of fruit purée you use.

YOU WILL NEED:

INGREDIENTS

- 2 cups strawberries, washed, dried, and stems removed
- ½ cup granulated sugar
- zest of ½ lemon
- 1 cup whole milk
- 4 large egg yolks
- ½ cup superfine sugar
- 1 ¼ cups whipping cream

EQUIPMENT

- blender, food processor or hand blender
- medium saucepan
- dish towel
- 2 medium bowls
- hand electric mixer
- spatula
- strainer
- wooden spoon
- large metal spoon
- freezer-proof container with a lid

OTHER GOOD FRUIT PURÉES TO USE INSTEAD OF STRAWBERRIES
- ✔ raspberries
- ✔ bananas
- ✔ mango
- ✔ peaches
- ✔ lightly cooked apricots
- ✔ stewed rhubarb
- ✔ blackberries
- ✔ stewed plums

1 Using a blender, blend the strawberries, granulated sugar, and lemon zest together into a smooth purée. Pour the mixture into a large bowl, cover, and chill in the refrigerator at least 1 hour.

2 To make the custard, follow the method on page 77 up to the end of point 5, but leave out the vanilla bean.

3 Once you have followed the method, wash and dry the beaters. Pour the cream into a medium bowl and beat until soft peaks form. Using a large metal spoon, quickly stir the custard into the strawberry purée.

4 Gently fold in the whipped cream. Pour the ice cream into the freezer-proof container. Put the lid on and freeze 4–5 hour, until it has frozen all around the edges.

5 Remove the ice cream from the container and put it into a food processor or blender, and process until smooth. This will remove all the ice crystals and make the ice cream easier to scoop. Pour it back into the container and freeze at least 6 hours. Take the ice cream out of the freezer 5 minutes before you want to eat it.

whisking cream

Cream should be whisked until soft peaks form. Be careful not to overwhip it, because once you've gone past the soft peak stage you'll never be able to get it back. Try making this Pavlova for your friends for your next birthday celebration.

pink birthday Pavlova

SERVES 8

YOU WILL NEED:

INGREDIENTS
- a knob of butter, for greasing
- 4 large egg whites (see page 63 on separating egg whites)
- 1 1/3 cups superfine sugar
- a pinch of salt
- 2 heaped teaspoons cornstarch
- 1 teaspoon vinegar
- 1 teaspoon vanilla extract
- 1–2 teaspoons red food coloring

for the filling:
- 1 1/4 cups whipping cream
- 1/2 lb raspberries
- 2 oz milk chocolate, grated (see page 69)
- 2 oz white chocolate, grated
- a handful of fresh mint leaves

EQUIPMENT
- grater
- baking sheet
- baking parchment
- pencil
- large plate
- large mixing bowl
- electric hand-held whisk
- metal spoon
- spatula
- palette knife
- oven gloves

1 Turn the oven on to 300°F.

2 Rub a little butter all over a baking sheet and line it with baking parchment. Use a pencil to draw a circle around a large plate on the paper.

3 Put the egg whites in a large mixing bowl and beat until stiff (see page 63). Then beat in the sugar a spoonful at a time, beating well between each spoonful. Then beat in the salt. They should be glossy and stiff enough for you to turn the bowl upside down without them falling out.

4 Quickly beat in the cornstarch, vinegar, vanilla extract, and food coloring.

5 Use a spatula to scrape the mixture out of the bowl into the circle on the paper. Use a palette knife to smooth the top.

6 Using oven gloves, put the Pavlova into the oven and immediately turn the oven down to 225°F. Cook 1 hour, then turn the oven off and leave the Pavlova to cool in the oven.

7 Take the Pavlova out of the oven. To lift the Pavlova off the paper, slide a palette knife between the paper and the baking sheet. Slide your hand underneath the paper and lift the Pavlova up a little, then peel half the paper off. Put the Pavlova on to a plate, slide a palette knife under the half with paper underneath, and gently pull the paper out. Or leave the Pavlova on the paper and just use a palette knife to lift off each slice of meringue.

8 Wash and dry the beaters and mixing bowl. Pour the cream into the bowl and whip until stiff. Spoon the whipped cream over the Pavlova. Scatter over the raspberries and chocolate. Decorate with a few mint leaves.

milkshakes, smoothies, and lassis

Milkshakes and smoothies are fun to make and so easy! You can use pretty much any fruit and mix it with either fruit juice or milk and yogurt. Just make sure the fruit is as ripe as possible to get maximum flavor. You will need a blender to help mix your ingredients into a smooth drink. I tend to use my hand blender, partly because it requires hardly any washing after using. Just remember to put the fruit and liquid into a tall container and push your blender blade right down to the bottom to avoid mess! Alternatively, throw all the ingredients into a blender or food processor and purée; you should only have a bowl and lid to wash afterward. You only need a juicer if you are making fresh fruit or vegetable juice, which I have avoided here for that very reason.

banana and peanut butter milkshake

SERVES 4

YOU WILL NEED:
INGREDIENTS
- 2 very ripe bananas (those with black spots are fine)
- 2 ⅓ cups milk
- 2 tablespoons smooth peanut butter
- 1 teaspoons honey

EQUIPMENT
- blender or food processor
- 4 glasses

1 Peel the bananas and then remove any stringy bits. Break the fruit into small pieces.

2 Put the bananas into a blender or food processor and then add all of the other ingredients.

3 Put the lid on and blend until smooth and frothy. Turn the blender off and leave it for a moment before removing the lid.

4 Pour the milkshake into 4 glasses. Serve immediately or the banana will start to go brown.

blueberry and ice cream shake

SERVES 4

YOU WILL NEED:
INGREDIENTS
- 2 ¾ cups blueberries
- 1 ¼ cups milk
- 6 small scoops of vanilla ice cream

EQUIPMENT
- blender or food processor
- ice cream scoop
- 4 glasses

1 Put the blueberries, milk, and 2 small scoops of ice cream into a blender or food processor.

2 Put the lid on and blend 2 minutes until smooth.

3 Turn the blender off and leave it for a moment before removing the lid.

4 Pour into 4 glasses and top each one with a small scoop of ice cream. Serve immediately or the blueberries will start to go brown.

milkshakes, smoothies, and lassis

thick strawberry smoothie
SERVES 4

YOU WILL NEED:
INGREDIENTS
- 1 small ripe banana
- 1 ⅔ cups frozen strawberries
- ⅔ cup fresh orange juice
- 6 heaped tablespoons natural yogurt

EQUIPMENT
- blender or food processor
- 4 glasses

1 Peel the banana and remove any stringy bits. Break it into small pieces.

2 Put the banana into a blender or food processor and add all the other ingredients.

3 Put the lid on and blend until smooth—you may need to stop the blender and push everything down before blending again to make sure the smoothie is really smooth.

4 Turn the blender off and leave it for a moment before removing the lid.

5 Pour into 4 glasses. Serve immediately or the banana will start to go brown.

pineapple and mint refresher
SERVES 4

YOU WILL NEED:
INGREDIENTS
- 1 medium ripe pineapple or 14 oz drained canned pineapple
- 1 ¼ cups freshly squeezed orange juice
- 6 large mint leaves
- ice cubes, to serve

EQUIPMENT
- chopping board
- serrated knife
- small knife
- blender or food processor
- large pitcher

1 If you are using fresh pineapple, put it on a chopping board and, using a serrated knife, slice off its top and bottom. Stand the fruit on one end.

2 Holding the top of it in one hand and the knife in the other, cut away a thin section of the skin following the curve of the fruit. Turn the fruit slightly and cut away another strip. Continue until you have peeled the pineapple all the way around.

3 If there are any "eyes" (little scratchy brown round bits) left, chop them out with a small knife. Cut the pineapple into chunks.

4 Put the pineapple into the blender and add the orange juice and mint. Put the lid on and blend 2 minutes until it is smooth. Turn the blender off and leave it for a moment before removing the lid.

5 Serve in a large pitcher with lots of ice cubes. It will keep for up to 24 hours in the refrigerator.

milkshakes, smoothies, and lassis

chocolate milkshake

SERVES 2

YOU WILL NEED:
INGREDIENTS
- 1 ¼ cups milk
- 2 heaped tablespoons sweetened cocoa powder
- 4 ice cubes
- 2 scoops chocolate ice cream (optional)

EQUIPMENT
- small saucepan
- blender or food processor
- plastic sandwich bag
- rolling pin
- ice cream scoop
- 4 glasses

1 Put ⅓ cup of the milk in a small saucepan. Put the rest of the milk back in the coldest part of the refrigerator.

2 Heat the saucepan over a gentle heat until the milk just starts to simmer.

3 Pour the hot milk into the blender. Sprinkle over the chocolate powder and put the lid on. Blend 1 minute until the powder has dissolved.

4 Put the ice in a plastic bag and hit with a rolling pin until there are no big bits left.

5 Take the lid off the blender and add the cold milk, crushed ice, and ice cream if you are using it. Put the lid back on, hold it on firmly and blend 2 minutes until smooth and frothy. Turn the blender off and leave it for a moment before you take off the lid.

6 Pour into 4 glasses and serve immediately.

mango lassi

SERVES 4

YOU WILL NEED:
INGREDIENTS
- 1 ripe mango (approx. 1 x 1 ¼ lbs mango or 14 ounces peeled flesh)
- 1 cup plain yogurt
- ½ cup milk
- ¼ cup cold water
- 2 teaspoons superfine sugar
- 4 ice cubes, plus 8 for serving

EQUIPMENT
- chopping board
- knife
- blender or food processor
- plastic sandwich bag
- rolling pin
- 4 glasses

1 To cut the flesh from the mango, hold it upright on a chopping board and, using a sharp knife, cut down either side of the pit, as close to it as possible. Peel off the skin and cut the flesh into large pieces. Trim any of the remaining fruit away from the pit, and put all the flesh into a blender or food processor.

2 Add the yogurt, milk, cold water, and sugar.

3 Put the ice cubes in a plastic bag and hit with a rolling pin until there are no big bits left. Tip the ice into the blender.

4 Put the lid on the blender and blend 2 minutes until smooth. Turn the blender off and leave it for a moment before you take off the lid.

5 Pour the lassi into 4 glasses, with a couple of ice cubes in each. It will keep up to 24 hours in the refrigerator.

white sauce

One of the first things chefs learn is how to make a white sauce, because it is used in so many dishes. And that's the brilliant thing about this technique—learn it and you've suddenly got loads more choices for dinner.

chicken, corn, and leek pie with sweet potato mash

SERVES 4

YOU WILL NEED:
INGREDIENTS
- 1 ¾ lbs sweet potatoes, peeled and cut into even-sized pieces
- ½ stick butter, plus a little extra
- 3 leeks, finely sliced (see page 100)
- ½ cup all-purpose flour
- 1 ⅔ cups milk
- a handful of chopped fresh parsley
- a pinch of salt and freshly ground black pepper
- 1 lb cooked chicken
- 1 ½ cups frozen corn, thawed, or canned and drained

EQUIPMENT
- vegetable peeler
- 2 knives
- large and medium saucepan
- colander and potato masher
- wooden spoon
- large pie dish
- baking sheet
- oven gloves

1 Bring a large pan of water to a boil. Add the potatoes and cook until tender. Drain in a colander. Return to the pan, add half of the butter and, using a potato masher, mash until smooth. Keep warm.

2 Turn the oven on to 350°F. Melt the remaining butter in a medium pan. Add the leeks and fry over a gentle heat until soft (this will take about 5 minutes). Add the flour and cook over a gentle heat 2 minutes, stirring constantly with a wooden spoon.

3 Take the pan off the heat and gradually add the milk, whisking all the time until you have a thick, smooth sauce (see step 3, page 87). Stir in the parsley, salt, and pepper.

4 Cut the chicken into bite-size chunks and stir into the sauce. Stir in the corn. Spoon the sauce into a large pie dish. Spoon the warm sweet potato mash on top. Dot a little extra butter over the top. Put the dish on to a baking sheet.

5 Using oven gloves, put the dish into the oven and cook 20–25 minutes until the potato is slightly golden and the pie is piping hot all the way through. Using oven gloves, take the pie out of the oven.

white sauce

macaroni cheese

SERVES 4

Macaroni cheese is one of my favorite recipes using white sauce.

YOU WILL NEED:

INGREDIENTS

- ½ stick unsalted butter
- ½ cup all-purpose flour
- 1 ¼ cups whole milk
- 1 ⅔ cups grated medium or mature Cheddar cheese (see page 69)
- a pinch of salt and freshly ground black pepper
- 10 oz macaroni pasta

EQUIPMENT

- cheese grater
- small saucepan
- wooden spoon
- large saucepan
- long-handled wooden spoon
- fork
- colander
- ovenproof dish
- spatula
- baking sheet
- oven gloves

1 Turn the oven on to 350°F. Put the butter in a small pan and melt it over a gentle heat; do not overheat it or let it brown because this will affect the colour and flavor of the sauce.

2 Ⓐ Add the flour and cook 1 minute, stirring constantly with a wooden spoon to make a smooth glossy paste.

3 Take the pan off the heat and add 2 tablespoons of milk. Stir until the milk is mixed in—he mixture will go very thick, but mix until it is smooth. Add a little more milk and stir again. Continue like this until you have used all the milk, mixing well between additions to stop your sauce from going lumpy.

4 Ⓑ Return the pan to a low heat and cook the sauce gently 5–6 minutes, whisking constantly. Remove from the heat; you should have a sauce of "pouring consistency." Stir in ¾ of the cheese. Add the salt and pepper.

5 Fill a large saucepan three-quarters full with cold water. Bring it to a boil over a high heat. Add a pinch of salt and the macaroni and stir well. Cook the macaroni for as long as it recommends on the package, keeping it at a good rolling boil and stirring occasionally (it should take 8–10 minutes).

6 Use a fork to take a piece of macaroni from the pan, leave it to cool slightly, then taste—it should be cooked but still have a little bite. Drain it in a colander and shake the colander.

7 Return the macaroni to the large saucepan, add the sauce, and mix well. Spoon it into an ovenproof dish, using a spatula to scrape out the sauce. Sprinkle over the remaining cheese and put the dish on to a baking sheet.

8 Using oven gloves, put the baking sheet and dish into the oven. Cook 15–20 minutes until the top is golden and the sauce is bubbling around the edges. Using oven gloves, take it out of the oven.

rubbing butter into flour

When rubbing butter into flour for crumbles, cookies, or pastry, all the ingredients need to be kept as cold as possible so that the butter does not melt in the flour and turn into a sticky mess. Your aim is to make coarse, not fine, breadcrumbs.

blackberry and apple crumble

SERVES 4

Making crumble is a great way to practice rubbing butter into flour. Unlike some crumbles, which can be a bit stodgy, this one is crisp. It is delicious served with custard sauce or thick yogurt.

YOU WILL NEED:

INGREDIENTS
- 1 stick butter, chilled, plus a knob for greasing
- 1 ½ cups all-purpose flour
- ½ level teaspoon cinnamon
- ⅓ cup light soft brown sugar

for the filling:
- 3 cups blackberries (or raspberries)
- 4 medium cooking apples, peeled, cored, and thinly sliced (see page 118)
- juice and zest of 1 small orange
- 3 tablespoons light brown sugar
- 1 level tablespoon all-purpose flour
- custard sauce or thick natural yogurt, to serve

EQUIPMENT
- vegetable peeler
- knife
- ovenproof dish
- flour sifter
- 2 large mixing bowls
- table knife
- spatula
- oven gloves

1 Turn the oven on to 400°F. Rub a little butter all over an ovenproof dish.

2 Hold the sifter high above a large mixing bowl and sift the flour and cinnamon into it.

3 Cut the butter into small pieces and stir into the flour. **A** To rub the butter into the flour, dip your fingertips into the flour and gently rub the pieces of butter between the tips of your thumbs and fingers so they flatten and gradually mix into the flour. Keep lifting your hands above the rim of the bowl, because this will let air get to the flour and keep the mixture cool.

4 Gently shake the bowl occasionally to make bits of butter come to the surface so you can rub them in. Keep rubbing until you can't see any more chunks of butter and the mixture looks like coarse breadcrumbs. Do this as quickly as possible, because the longer you touch the butter the hotter it will become, and your mixture may become greasy. If this happens, put it in the refrigerator for 5 minutes and then continue. Stir in the sugar.

5 Put the fruit into a large bowl. Sprinkle over the orange juice, zest, sugar, and flour and mix gently using your hands. Tip everything into the buttered dish, scraping out the bowl with a spatula. Spread it in the dish.

6 **B** Using your hand, sprinkle the crumble mixture on top of the fruit and spread it out so all the fruit is covered. Using oven gloves, put the dish into the oven and bake 25–30 minutes until the crumble top is crisp and the blackberry juices are bubbling up around the edges.

7 Use oven gloves to take the dish out of the oven and allow to cool for a few minutes before serving with custard sauce or thick natural yogurt.

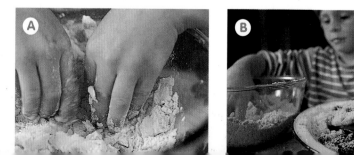

french fries

I tend to make french fries in the oven instead of frying them for several reasons: They are better for you, they are easier to cook, and you are not left with a smelly kitchen. However, if you decide to deep-fry them, there are a few guidelines to follow. Peel the potatoes and cut them into sticks about ½ inch wide and 2 inches long. Keep the potatoes in a bowl of water until you are ready to cook them, but drain and pat them dry before cooking. Corn oil is good for deep-frying, and should be heated in a large saucepan or fryer to 325°F. Cook some fries at this temperature 4–6 minutes, lift them out of the oil, then turn the heat up to 375°F. Return them to the pan and cook a further 2–3 minutes until golden brown. Drain on paper towels. These steps insure that the potatoes are soft and fluffy on the inside and crisped to perfection on the outside. Always ask an adult to help you when making french fries.

chunky oven fries

SERVES 4

YOU WILL NEED:

INGREDIENTS
- 4 large baking potatoes
- 3 tablespoons corn oil
- 2 teaspoons paprika (optional)
- ⅔ cup sour cream
- 3 tablespoons barbecue sauce

EQUIPMENT
- vegetable scrubbing brush
- chopping board
- knife and large roasting pan
- dish towel and oven gloves
- fish turner and small bowl

OTHER THINGS TO DO WITH FRENCH FRIES
- ✔ as an alternative dip, mix lots of chopped herbs into sour cream and leave out the paprika and barbecue sauce
- ✔ try serving the chunky fries with guacamole or salsa

1 Turn the oven on to 400°F. Scrub the potatoes under running water to remove any dirt and cut out any potato eyes with a knife.

2 **A** Put the potatoes on a chopping board and, using a knife, cut each potato in half lengthwise, then in half again, then again, so each is cut into 8. Put the oil in the roasting pan and, using oven gloves, place in the oven.

3 Dry the wedges on a dish towel. Using oven gloves, remove the pan from the oven after 5 minutes and quickly add the potatoes (the oil will be hot). **B** Sprinkle on the paprika. Using oven gloves, put the pan in the oven.

4 Cook 10 minutes. Using oven gloves, take the tray out of the oven. Use a fish turner to turn the fries over so they brown evenly. Using oven gloves, put them back in the oven for 10 minutes.

5 Put the sour cream and barbecue sauce into a bowl and mix. Using oven gloves, take the potatoes out of the oven. Using the fish turner, lift them into a serving dish and serve with the dip.

boiling potatoes

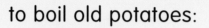

to boil old potatoes:

1 Scrub large old potatoes, round white varieties are best, under cold running water.

2 Use a vegetable peeler to peel the potatoes—most of the nutrients are just under the skin so you want to try and peel them as thinly as possible. Use the end of the peeler to remove any obvious bad bits or green bits.

3 Put the potatoes on to a chopping board and cut into even-size pieces— this usually means cutting each potato into about 3 pieces. Doing this will insure the potatoes cook evenly in the same amount of time.

4 Half fill a saucepan with water, cover with a lid, and bring to a boil.  **A** Add a small pinch of salt (optional; I don't add salt) and add the potatoes.

5 Bring back to a boil, then turn down the heat so the water is simmering. Cover with a lid, leaving a small gap for the steam to escape and cook 15–20 minutes or until they are tender—this will depend on the size of your potatoes. Carefully lift the lid off using your oven gloves and watch out for hot steam. **B** Test the largest potato with a knife—if it slides in easily and the potatoes feel tender, then they are ready.

6 Turn the heat off and place a colander in the sink. Using your oven gloves carefully take the pan to the sink. Drain the potatoes and leave for a minute so they dry out. Tip into a serving dish or use for mashed potatoes (see page 96).

to boil new potatoes:

1 New potatoes are usually small, with a papery skin that does not need to be peeled. Most of it can be scrubbed off when you wash the potatoes. Scrub evenly sized new potatoes, under cold running water—using a vegetable scrubbing brush is easiest. Make sure you remove any bits of mud or grit and as much skin as you can. Rinse them well.

2 Put the potatoes on to a chopping board. If there are any that are much bigger than the rest, cut them in half.

3 Cook as above in points 4 to 6, adding a sprig of mint to the potatoes before boiling them.

4 Once you've drained them, throw away the mint and serve the new potatoes with a knob of butter.

boiling potatoes

simple potato salad

SERVES 4

In this recipe the dressing for the salad is added while the potatoes are still warm. This means they will absorb much more flavor. You can eat the salad warm or at room temperature. This would be lovely with chicken kebabs and a big green salad.

YOU WILL NEED:

INGREDIENTS

- 1 ¾ lbs small new potatoes
- salt
- 1 tablespoon olive oil
- finely grated zest of 1 lemon
- freshly ground black pepper
- 3 tablespoons mayonnaise
- 3 tablespoons crème fraîche or Greek yogurt
- 1 tablespoon finely chopped parsley
- 1 tablespoon finely chopped chives

EQUIPMENT

- vegetable scrubbing brush
- knife
- chopping board
- medium saucepan
- colander
- oven gloves
- lemon zester
- wooden spoon
- large serving bowl

1 Scrub the potatoes under cold running water. Cut out any bruised or dark bits. If there are any potatoes much bigger than the rest cut them in half. This will insure that the potatoes cook evenly.

2 Three quarters fill a saucepan with water and bring to a boil. Carefully add the potatoes. Add a pinch of salt. Bring back to a boil and cook about 20 minutes—this will depend on the size of your potatoes. Test them by sticking a knife into the largest potato—it should feel tender.

3 Place a colander in the sink and using your oven gloves take the pan to the sink and drain the potatoes, then tip them back into the hot pan.

4 Add the olive oil and lemon zest. Season with salt and freshly ground black pepper. Stir the potatoes gently so they are all covered with the oil. Leave to cool about 10 minutes.

5 Put the mayonnaise, crème fraîche, or Greek yogurt and herbs into a serving bowl and mix together well. Add the cooled potatoes and stir gently.

boiling potatoes

mashed potatoes

SERVES 4–6

Mashed potatoes are one of the easiest things to make, but the most important thing to remember is to choose the right potato. Potatoes have different textures, some are "floury" and some "waxy." Waxy potatoes are great for salads, but make terrible mashed potatoes, whereas floury potatoes, which go light and fluffy when cooked, are perfect for mash.

YOU WILL NEED:

INGREDIENTS
- 2 lbs floury potatoes, such as Russet
- ½ cup whole milk
- ½ stick butter
- salt and freshly ground black pepper
- a pinch of ground nutmeg (optional)

EQUIPMENT
- vegetable peeler
- chopping board
- knife
- medium saucepan with lid
- colander
- oven gloves
- wooden spoon
- potato masher

GOOD THINGS TO ADD TO MASH
- ✔ for Italian-style mash, crush a garlic clove and fry it in a big knob of butter until very pale golden. Add to the mash along with 1¾ oz of freshly grated Parmesan
- ✔ 2 tbsp of red or green pesto – great with grilled or roast chicken
- ✔ 2 tbsp of mint sauce or jelly – try serving minty mash with roast lamb or grilled lamb chops
- ✔ 1¾oz grated Cheddar or other hard cheese
- ✔ 1 tsp of grainy mustard – delicious with pork chops
- ✔ chopped fresh herbs
- ✔ cooked chopped leeks, red onion or spinach
- ✔ crumbled crispy bacon

1 Peel the potatoes with a vegetable peeler (see page 94, point 2). If your potatoes are very large cut them in half, so that all the pieces are roughly the same size. This will insure the potatoes cook evenly.

2 Boil the potatoes until they are tender, then drain them in a colander.

3 Return the potatoes to the hot saucepan and using your oven gloves put the saucepan back on to the heat. Turn the heat on low for one minute and keep moving the potatoes around with a wooden spoon—this will help to dry them out and make the mash really fluffy. Turn the heat off and add the milk and butter. Stir with the wooden spoon until the butter is melted then go in with your potato masher.

4 Mash as hard as you can, moving the masher all around the pan until you get rid of all the lumps, and the milk and butter are all mixed in. When the potatoes are smooth and fluffy, season them with salt and pepper and, if you like, add a little bit of ground nutmeg—this gives the potatoes a lovely flavor.

5 You can also mash an equal quantity of other boiled or steamed vegetables, such as carrots, parsnips, rutabaga, or celeriac.

slicing and chopping vegetables

tomato sauce with fresh basil

SERVES 4

If your pasta sauce is a bit thick, drain the pasta but reserve a little of the cooking water and stir it into the sauce to give it a better consistency. You could also try scattering over some torn mozzarella before serving.

YOU WILL NEED:

INGREDIENTS
- 1 small red onion
- 3 tbsp olive oil
- 2 garlic cloves, peeled and crushed
- 3 cups canned chopped plum tomatoes
- ½ lb ripe plum tomatoes, chopped
- salt and freshly ground black pepper
- a pinch of sugar
- handful of fresh basil leaves, torn
- ¾ lb spaghetti

EQUIPMENT
- garlic press
- knife
- chopping board
- medium saucepan
- wooden spoon
- large saucepan
- long-handled wooden spoon
- colander
- oven gloves
- serving dish

1 Cut the onion in half and remove the papery outer leaves. Lay it outside down on the chopping board and chop it finely (see page 100).

2 Heat the oil in a saucepan until it is just starting to get hot. Add the garlic and onion and sauté gently 7–9 minutes, stirring occasionally with a wooden spoon, until the onions are soft and transparent.

3 Add the canned and fresh chopped tomatoes. Season with salt and pepper and add a pinch of sugar and half the basil leaves. Cook 15 minutes, stirring occasionally. Remove from the heat.

4 Three quarters fill a large saucepan—the largest one you can find— with water. Add 2 teaspoons of salt. Bring to a boil.

5 Carefully put the spaghetti into the pan, wait a moment for it to soften, then use a long-handled wooden spoon to push the spaghetti down into the water.

6 Bring back to a boil and cook according to the package instructions.

7 When it is done (see page 87, point 6), use your oven gloves to take the pan to the sink and drain the pasta in a colander. Since the pan may be heavy, you might want to ask an adult for help with this. Immediately tip the hot pasta back into the pan, pour over the tomato sauce, and add more torn basil reserving some for the final dish. Give it a really good stir and pour it into a warm serving dish. Tear the basil roughly and scatter over the pasta. Serve immediately.

slicing and chopping vegetables

red bell peppers

A Lay the pepper on the chopping board, hold it firmly, and slice all the way through the middle, cutting through the green stalk at one end. Carefully scrape out all the seeds and cut away the white membrane. Cut each piece in half and lay them skin side down on the chopping board. If you need slices, just cut each piece one way as thick or as thin as you like. If you need dice cut it into long strips, then turn the strips and cut them the other way into big or small cubes, according to your recipe.

onions

Hold the onion firmly in one hand and carefully slice it in half, aiming the knife through the middle of the root at the bottom of the onion. Leaving the root on will help keep the onion together while you slice it. Peel the papery skin from the onion. To slice the onion, lay it cut side down on the chopping board. Slice the edge of the onion as thinly as you can until you have worked your way to the other side of the onion. Carefully chop the root off, and use your hand to spread the onion out. Repeat with the other half of the onion. **B** To chop the onion, slice the onion exactly as described above but do not chop the root off. Hold the onion firmly in one hand and use your knife to cut slices across it the other way so it forms little cubes. Keep going until you reach the root. As you near the root, tuck the tips of your fingers under so that the knife does not catch them. Throw the root away. Repeat with the second half of the onion.

leeks

Slice the leek in half all the way along from the dark green at the top to the white bit at the root. Remove the tough outer leaves. Clean the leek really well under cold running water, checking between the layers for mud and grit. Lay it cut side down on a chopping board and slice it finely across starting at the dark green end and working down to the root. Throw the root bit away.

herbs, e.g. parsley, cilantro, chives

Wash the herbs and pat them dry on paper towels. Remove any really coarse stems or bad bits. Use your hand to draw the herbs into a tight bunch on the chopping board and cut through them with the knife chopping as close together as possible. Gather all the herbs together again and chop through them again. Then hold the handle of the knife in one hand and the top of the pointed end in the other. Hold the pointed end steady in the same position and move the knife blade in a rocking motion backwards and forwards over the herbs until they are finely chopped.

puréeing soup

Puréed soup is where the vegetables are forced through a strainer, or liquidized using a food processor or blender to give a smooth but thick liquid. If you have never used a piece of equipment, always ask to be shown how to use it before you try yourself.

food processor

First get an adult to help you attach the bowl and blade correctly. Let the soup cool slightly and using a large ladle, ladle the soup into the food processor. Never fill it to the top—about three-quarters full is best, because when you turn the processor on the soup will rise up. Put the lid on, making sure it clicks firmly closed and press the pulse button. Blend until the soup is smooth—food processors are quite powerful so this will only take a minute or two. If there are any big lumps you may need to use a wooden spoon to push them down, then put the lid back on and process again. Take the lid off and carefully remove the blade holding the plastic center—remember the metal blades are very sharp. Remove the bowl from the machine and pour the soup back into the saucepan to be reheated.

hand blender

This is one of the quickest ways to purée soup because you purée it in the pan that it is cooked in. Let the soup cool a little then put the pan on a folded dish towel so that it won't move. If the blender has a speed control set it to the middle speed. Holding the blender upright put it right down into the bottom of the pan, making sure the blade is completely under the surface. This will insure that when you turn it on the soup will not spurt out. Hold the blender steadily and press the pulse button. If there are big lumps you may need to lift it up and down or stir it about to get the soup smooth—when you do this, always stop pressing the pulse button so you do not get splashed. If you are using a deep saucepan, try tilting the blender slightly so that it sucks up and blends the lumps.

liquidizer/blender

Make sure the container is firmly attached to the base. If you are not sure, ask an adult to help you. Use a soup ladle to ladle the soup into the container. Never fill it more than three-quarters full, or it will spill when you turn the blender on. Put the lid on firmly and cover the top of the blender with a folded dish towel. This means any small leaks will not splash. Turn the blender on and blend until the soup is smooth. Wait until the motor has stopped completely before you remove the lid. Never try to stir it while the motor is running. Pour the soup back into the saucepan to be reheated.

mouli or moulinette

A mouli is a kind of metal strainer that sits over a bowl or pan. It has an attachable blade that you turn by hand, and you can use it to purée any kind of soft fruit, vegetables, soups, etc. It usually comes with a set of different metal plates—this means you can purée things coarsely or finely. For this soup use a metal plate with medium-size holes. Put a bowl on to a dish towel and sit the mouli over it. Ladle some of the soup into it and turn the handle backward and forward until the liquid has gone down, then ladle in more soup. Keep going until all the soup has gone and you have gotten as much through the mouli as possible. Carefully pour the soup back into the saucepan to be reheated.

strainer

If you are really stuck and don't have any of the above equipment you can always purée a soup by pushing it through a strainer with a wooden spoon—it may take longer but your soup will be just as yummy!

puréeing soup

carrot and butternut squash soup with honey croûtons

SERVES 6

This is a good thing to make if you want to practice chopping vegetables. The main thing to remember when you are cutting up vegetables that all go into the same dish is to try and make them roughly the same size. That way when the soup is simmering they will all cook in the same amount of time.

YOU WILL NEED:

INGREDIENTS
- ½ stick butter
- 1 small onion, peeled and chopped
- 1 small garlic clove, peeled and crushed
- 6 medium carrots, peeled and chopped
- 1 large potato, peeled and chopped
- 1 medium butternut squash—approx. 2 ¼ lbs, peeled, deseeded, and chopped
- 4 cups vegetable or chicken stock
- juice of ½ orange
- 1 crusty white roll
- 1 tablespoon runny honey
- 1 tablespoon olive oil

EQUIPMENT
- chopping board
- knife
- garlic press
- large saucepan
- wooden spoon
- oven gloves
- blender, food processor, or hand blender
- serrated knife
- baking sheet

1 Melt the butter in a large saucepan over a low heat. Add the onion, garlic, and carrot and cook about 5 minutes, stirring occasionally with a wooden spoon, until the onion is soft and looks almost transparent.

2 Add the potato and cook a few more minutes, stirring often.

3 Add the butternut squash and cook 4 more minutes, stirring often to make sure the vegetables don't stick to the bottom of the pan.

4 Pour over the stock and orange juice and turn up the heat. Stir well and bring the soup to a boil. Reduce the heat and simmer 25 minutes until the vegetables are soft. Turn the oven on to 400°F.

5 Using oven gloves take the pan off the heat. **A** and **B** Let it cool for a few minutes, then ladle into a food processor or blender and purée until the soup is smooth (see page 101).

6 Cut the roll in half with a serrated knife. Cut each half into strips and cut those into small cubes. Put them on to a baking sheet. Drizzle over the honey and oil. Use your hands to gently mix them so they are all equally coated, then spread them out evenly.

7 Using oven gloves, put the baking sheet into the oven and cook 6–8 minutes until the croûtons are golden. Use oven gloves to remove the tray from the oven.

8 Put the soup back on the hob and heat it gently through. You may need to add some hot water to thin the soup to the consistency that you like. Serve the soup with the honey croûtons.

roasting vegetables

You can roast a variety of vegetables. There are a few guidelines to bear in mind. Choose similar types of vegetables to roast together. For example, Mediterranean-style vegetables, such as eggplant, zucchini, bell peppers, tomatoes, and onions, all taste good together. Similarly, root vegetables, such as rutabaga, sweet potato, celeriac, and butternut squash, are wonderful cooked together. To make sure that the vegetables cook evenly, you will need to cut them into evenly size pieces. Then drizzle with a good tasty oil, such as olive oil, and seasonings, such as herbs and garlic, and roast at a high temperature 30–40 minutes.

roasted Mediterranean vegetables

SERVES 4

YOU WILL NEED:

INGREDIENTS
- 1 lb tomatoes
- 1 small eggplant
- 2 medium zucchini
- 1 small red bell pepper
- 1 red onion and 2 garlic cloves
- 3 tablespoons olive oil

EQUIPMENT
- chopping board and oven gloves
- knife, garlic press, and fish turner
- large heavy-based roasting pan

TRY ROASTING
✔ scrubbed new potatoes with oil and garlic and serve them with roast chicken or with a good dollop of sour cream
✔ corn on the cob and serve with a knob of plain or flavored butter (butter with a little chopped chili and cilantro would be really good)
✔ a mixture of butternut squash, red onion, carrots, and sweet potato and serve with broiled pork chops or roast chicken
✔ big tomatoes or plum tomatoes. Just cut them in half and put them cut side up in the pan. Drizzle with oil, crushed garlic, and salt and pepper. Serve them warm or cold with crusty bread

1 Turn the oven on to 400°F.

2 **A** Chop the tomatoes into halves or quarters and put them in the roasting pan. Cut the eggplant and zucchini into bite-size pieces and add to the pan. Cut the bell pepper in half and remove the seeds, then cut it into bite-size pieces. Cut the onion in half, remove the skin, and cut each half into 4 wedges, leaving the root on so the wedges don't fall apart during cooking. Add to the other vegetables.

3 Peel the garlic and crush in a garlic press and sprinkle over the vegetables. Drizzle over the olive oil and season well with salt and freshly ground black pepper.

4 Use your hands to mix everything together really well so that all the vegetables are coated in oil and garlic.

5 Using your oven gloves put the roasting pan into the oven and roast the vegetables 20 minutes. Wearing your oven gloves, carefully remove the pan from the oven and use a fish turner to turn the vegetables over. Put the pan back in the oven and cook a further 15–20 minutes until the vegetables are just beginning to crisp and go golden around the edges.

growing herbs

If you have a garden and you are able to grow a few things in a small patch somewhere, then make the most of it. It is so exciting to see something grow from a seed into a plant, especially if you can then eat the plant too. Or if you only have a windowsill, don't despair, because there are still plenty of things that you can grow.

Have you tasted fresh herbs in your food? Do you like the taste of fresh mint, or parsley, or chives, or cilantro? Herbs can add so much flavor and color to dishes, but they can be expensive to buy. If you can grow some herbs yourself, you can end up with a pot of herbs on your windowsill for a number of weeks—especially if the pots are kept by a sunny window.

You will need:
• a large handful of small stones;
• a plant pot (or just poke two or three holes in the bottom of a large yogurt or margarine pot);
• potting soil and a saucer;
• some seeds—buy a package from your local garden center, such as parsley, basil, chives, thyme, cilantro, or mint.

What you do:

1 Put a handful of small stones into the bottom of the pot.
2 Half fill the pot with soil and put the pot on to a saucer.
3 Sprinkle the seeds over the soil and cover with more soil. Make sure that you read the directions on the seed package.
4 Label the pot so that you know what herbs you are growing.
5 Water lightly and keep the soil moist until the seeds start to grow.
6 Then for the really exciting bit— watch them grow!
7 Water your herbs when the soil feels dry when you touch it.
8 Pinch or snip off the tops of herbs with scissors when you need some —the herbs will grow back.

If you want to plant your herbs outside, wait until they have grown to at least 3–4 inches tall, but make sure there is no chance of any ground frost occuring in the near future in your garden. Then you can either leave them in their pot and put that straight into the ground or take them out of the pot and put the herbs straight into the ground. Some herbs, such as chives and mint, will come up again next year.

Herbs can be used for many things. Try adding them to salads or to dressings; sprinkling them into pasta sauces (see page 99); adding them to breadcrumbs to coat fish (see page 16); adding fresh mint to desserts, such as on top of the pink Pavlova (see page 81), or adding them to drinks, such as the pink lemonade (see page 121). Some of the more robust herbs, such as thyme and rosemary, can be dried and then kept in the kitchen in bundles to be used in cooking.

grow your own cress

One of the simplest things to grow is cress and it grows really quickly, so you will not have to wait too long for a result. There are many ways to grow cress, but I was taught to make a cress 'head', which I thought you might like to have a go at, too.

You will need:
• a yogurt pot;
• stickers or paper and glue;
• few sheets of kitchen paper;
• a handful of cotton wool;
• mustard and cress seeds.

What you do:

1 Wash the pot and remove the label.
2 Stick on some eyes, a nose and a mouth using stickers or make these with paper and glue.
3 Scrunch up the kitchen paper and put under the tap, wring out slightly so that it is not too wet. Put this inside the yogurt pot.
4 Put the cotton wool into some water to make it just damp then rest on top of the kitchen paper.
5 Sprinkle over a mixture of mustard and cress seeds and press them down lightly with your fingers.
6 Leave the pot in a warm light place.
7 Keep an eye on the cotton wool and if it seems dry add water.
8 You should see some growth after about 7 days. Eventually the cress will start to grow over the top of the pot and it will look like hair on top of the face that you drew.

herbs

green salad with tomatoes, mozzarella, and pesto croûtons

SERVES 4

The secret to making a good salad is to give it different textures and this one is especially delicious with its crisp croûtons, crunchy lettuce and soft mozzarella. It's really a meal in itself.

YOU WILL NEED:
INGREDIENTS

- 2 garlic cloves, peeled
- ⅓ cup pine nuts
- 2 oz basil leaves
- ⅔ cup olive oil, plus 4 tablespoons
- ½ stick soft unsalted butter
- 5 tablespoons Parmesan
- 2 ciabatta rolls
- 1 large romaine lettuce
- ½ lb cherry tomatoes
- 1 ripe avocado
- 6 oz fresh mozzarella

for the salad dressing:
- 3 tablespoons olive oil
- 1 tablespoon balsamic vinegar
- 1 tablespoon lemon juice
- pinch of dark brown sugar
- salt and freshly ground black pepper

EQUIPMENT
- knife and palette knife
- chopping board
- baking sheet and oven gloves
- salad spinner or dish towel
- large salad bowl and screw-top jar
- teaspoon

OTHER GOOD THINGS TO ADD TO THIS SALAD
- ✔ crispy bits of cooked bacon
- ✔ cooked cold chicken, torn into strips
- ✔ a little grated Parmesan or some toasted pine nuts

1 First make the pesto. Using a pestle and mortar (or if you do not have one a food processor), pound the garlic with ½ teaspoon salt and pine nuts until broken up. Add the basil leaves a few at a time and continue to pound. Beat in the olive oil little by little until the mixture is thick and creamy. Beat in the butter and finally the Parmesan. You can store this in a jar with a thin layer of oil on top—just remove the oil before using the pesto.

2 Turn the oven on to 400°F. Cut the ciabatta rolls in half, then cut them into small cubes. Put them on a baking sheet. Drizzle over the 4 tablespoons of olive oil and 2 tablespoons of the pesto and use your hands to mix it all together, so each piece is coated in oil and pesto.

3 Using oven gloves, put the tray in the oven and bake for 5 minutes. Using oven gloves, remove the tray from the oven and use a palette knife to turn the croûtons over. Return the tray to the oven and cook for 10 minutes. Using oven gloves, remove the tray from the oven and leave to cool.

4 Pull apart the lettuce, separating the leaves and cut away the tough root. Wash the lettuce under cold water and dry in a salad spinner. If you don't have a salad spinner, just dry the lettuce in a clean dish towel. Bring all the edges of the dish towel together so you have a little bag and take it outside. Hold tight, then swing the bag up and down and all the water will come out.

5 Put the lettuce leaves into a large salad bowl, tearing any large leaves into smaller pieces. Cut the tomatoes in half and add to the bowl. Cut the avocado in half and remove the pit. Use a teaspoon to scoop out the flesh into the salad bowl. Use your hands to tear off small bits of mozzarella into the salad bowl. The bits of avocado and mozzarella should be roughly the same size as the halved tomatoes.

6 To make the dressing put all the ingredients into a screw-top jar. Put the lid on tightly, then shake the jar until the dressing looks pale and is all mixed together. Open the jar and taste the dressing for seasoning.

7 Put the croûtons into the salad bowl and gently mix everything so the croûtons are evenly distributed—the easiest way to do this is to use your hands. Slowly drizzle the dressing over the salad and serve it immediately.

jam

Jams are made from crushed fruit and sugar. Pectin, a gum-like substance, found to some degree in all fruit, helps the jam to set so that it is not runny. Some fruits contain more pectin than others, and so will set more easily—for example, apples, quinces, plums, lemons, and oranges. Jam made from fruit, such as rhubarb, strawberries, and pears, may need to have some commercial pectin added or a little lemon juice to help make it set. Making jam is a great way to preserve lots of cheap, seasonal, fresh fruit. Since jam can get very hot, you may need to get an adult to help you make it.

raspberry jam

MAKES 6 X 10 OZ JAM JARS

YOU WILL NEED:
INGREDIENTS
- 3 lbs raspberries (or blackberries, blueberries)
- 3 lbs granulated sugar
- ½ cup cranberry juice

EQUIPMENT
- 6 x 10 oz jam jars with lids
- newspaper
- large roasting pan
- preserving pan or large heavy-based saucepan
- long-handled wooden spoon
- small saucer
- teaspoon
- oven gloves
- ladle
- 6 waxed paper disks
- 6 sticky labels and a pen

1 Take the lids off the washed empty jam jars. Lay a piece of newspaper in the bottom of a roasting pan and stand the jars on top. Turn the oven to 250°F and pop the jars into the oven.

2 Put the raspberries into a preserving pan or heavy-based saucepan and heat gently until they start to give up their juice, then bring to a boil. Boil 2–3 minutes. Add the sugar to the pan, then pour over the cranberry juice. Heat gently, stirring constantly until the sugar has dissolved—you can tell when this happens because the bottom of the pan will feel smooth when you stir. If it feels grainy the sugar is not yet dissolved.

3 Put a saucer into the refrigerator to use later, to test the jam's setting point.

4 When the sugar is dissolved, bring the jam up to a boil again. Boil approximately 12 minutes until the jam reaches setting point. You can test this with a sugar thermometer (see page 76). It should read 220°F —this temperature is often marked on the thermometer as "jam." If you do not have a sugar thermometer, spoon a little blob on to the cold saucer. As it cools it should start to set. **A** Push the jam with a teaspoon—the surface should wrinkle, which means it has reached setting point.

5 If the jam hasn't yet set, boil a further 5 minutes and test again. Keep doing this until it has set.

6 Using your oven gloves carefully remove the pan from the heat then remove the warmed glass jars from the oven. **B** Use a ladle to very carefully fill the jars with jam. Cover with waxed paper disks and leave to cool before putting the lids back on. Don't forget to label your jam with the date and the type of fruit you used!

using pop molds

You can buy plastic pop molds in most kitchenware stores or by mail order. If you don't have any, you can always use small plastic cups and spoons, don't use metal spoons for icepops because they will hurt your teeth when you eat the lolly! You could also use ice cube trays.

orange and passion fruit icepops

MAKES 4

You can make icepops out of almost anything that you would normally have as a cold drink. The pop molds I have used take 2 ¾ fl oz of liquid. Yours may take slightly more or less.

YOU WILL NEED:
INGREDIENTS
• 4 passion fruit
• 1 ½ cups orange juice

EQUIPMENT
• knife
• chopping board
• teaspoon
• strainer
• bowl
• wooden spoon
• pop molds and sticks, or plastic cups and spoons

1 Cut the passion fruit in half. **A** Using a teaspoon, scoop out the pulp from the passion fruit and strain it into a bowl using a wooden spoon to push through as much juice as you can. Add the orange juice to the passion fruit juice and stir. **B** Carefully pour the purée into 4 pop molds, filling them almost to the top. Don't fill them right up because the mixture will expand when it freezes. Carefully tap the molds on the work surface, so that any air bubbles pop to the top.

2 Carefully put the lids on and add the pop sticks. Put the pop molds into the freezer, making sure they are standing upright. Leave to freeze at least 6 hours or overnight until the icepops are completely solid.

3 When you want to eat the icepops, fill a bowl full of hot water. Dip the bottom of the pop molds into the water, being careful not to let the water come over the top. Hold the icepops in the hot water for about a minute then carefully pull them from the molds.

For raspberry icepops: put 1 cup of raspberries and 1 cup of cranberry juice into a food processor or blender and blend until smooth. If you don't like seeds, strain the purée. Carefully pour the mixture into the pop molds, and follow the method above.

For raspberry yogurt icepops: put ⅔ cup of fresh or frozen raspberries into a blender with 1 cup of raspberry yogurt and blend until smooth. Carefully pour the mixture into the pop molds, and follow the method above.

For apricot yogurt icepops: put ⅔ cup of canned apricots in syrup (drained) into a blender with 1 cup of apricot yogurt and blend until smooth. You may need to stop the blender and push everything down with a spatula before blending again to make sure the apricots are really smooth. Carefully pour the mixture into the pop molds, and follow the method above.

A

B

using jello molds

One of the best things about making jello is choosing a mold to put it in. Look for cheap plastic molds in a good kitchenware store—you will probably find small individual molds as well as large ones. Ask your grandma if she still has a glass or china jelly mold, because these used to be popular and often come in wonderful shapes. If you do use a china or glass mold you may need to grease it lightly with a little flavorless oil first. Alternatively, use a large glass or plastic bowl or small plastic cups instead. Wet the serving plate slightly before turning out your jello, so if it does not go on to the middle of the plate you can slide it into position.

berry fruit two-tone jello

MAKES 1 LARGE WOBBLY JELLO DESSERT

Experiment with the jello and add any fresh fruit that you like. Try and find a jello mold to give your jello a good old-fashioned shape, but if you don't have one, just use cups or bowls instead.

YOU WILL NEED:

INGREDIENTS
- 1 ⅔ cups summer fruit, such as strawberries, raspberries or blackberries
- 1 package of strawberry Jell-O
- 1 package of blackberry Jell-O

EQUIPMENT
- knife
- large sauce pan
- chopping board
- large bowl or jello mold that will hold 2 ½ pints of water
- kitchen scissors
- large pitcher
- wooden spoon
- plastic wrap
- dish towel
- plate

1 Pick over the fruit, removing any stems. If you are using strawberries, cut any large ones in half. Put the fruit into a large bowl or jello mold.

2 Put a large saucepan of water on to boil. Using kitchen scissors cut the strawberry Jell-O into pieces. Put it into a large pitcher and carefully pour over 1 cup of boiling water. Stir continuously until the jello is completely dissolved. Add 1 cup of cold water to the pitcher and stir well.

3 Leave to cool for 10 minutes then carefully pour the liquid jello over the fruit, all the fruit will float to the surface.

4 Leave to cool completely, then cover with plastic wrap and put into the refrigerator and leave to set—his will take about 2 hours, depending on how cold your refrigerator is.

5 When the strawberry jello is set make the next layer. Put the large saucepan with water on again. Chop the blackberry Jell-O into pieces using kitchen scissors and put into a clean large pitcher.

6 Carefully pour over 1 cup of boiling water. Stir continuously until the jello has completely dissolved. Add 1 cup of cold water to the pitcher and stir well. Leave to cool for 10 minutes.

7 Take the already set strawberry jello out of the refrigerator and remove the plastic wrap. Carefully pour over the blackberry jelly. Leave to cool completely, then cover with plastic wrap and put back into the refrigerator and leave until all the jello is completely set.

8 To turn it out, dip the bottom of the bowl into a sink full of hot water for a few seconds. Lift the bowl out and put it on to a dish towel. Put an upside down wet plate on the top of the bowl, then quickly turn it all over so the jello comes out neatly on to the plate. You may want to ask an adult to help you with this.

chopping fruit

chocolate fondue with tropical fruit

SERVES 4

Fruit often has less flavor when it's cold, especially soft summer fruit. Imagine the taste of a strawberry just picked, warm from the sun, and the taste of one that is cold from the refrigerator—there is no comparison! So, if you prepare the fruit for the fondue in advance, be sure to take it out of the refrigerator at least half an hour before you serve it. You don't have to use just tropical fruit; fruit such as strawberries, plums, apricots, or cherries are perfect for a summer fondue.

YOU WILL NEED:
INGREDIENTS
- ½ lb good quality bittersweet or milk chocolate
- ½ cup condensed milk
- ½ cup water

for the fruit:
- 1 ripe mango
- 1 large ripe banana
- 1 ripe papaya
- 2 cups small marshmallows
- large handful of fresh ripe strawberries

EQUIPMENT
- chopping board
- knife
- spoon
- large serving plate
- medium-size saucepan
- medium bowl
- wooden spoon
- oven gloves
- 2 small serving bowls
- forks or wooden skewers, for dipping

1 Cut the mango's flesh away from the pit, then peel (see page 118 on chopping mangoes and other fruit). Cut into bite-size chunks.

2 Peel the banana and cut into bite-size pieces.

3 Cut the papaya in half and scoop out the seeds with a spoon. Cut the pieces in half and using a sharp knife carefully peel away the skin. Cut the flesh into bite-size chunks.

4 Arrange all the fruit on a serving plate, leaving a space for the bowl of fondue. Put the fruit in the refrigerator if you are preparing it in advance.

5 Quarter fill a saucepan with water and bring to a boil. Break the chocolate into small pieces and put into a medium bowl. Pour over the condensed milk and water.

6 Rest the bowl over the saucepan and turn the heat right down. Stir gently with a wooden spoon until the chocolate has completely melted and the fondue is smooth.

7 Using oven gloves, carefully pour the fondue into a small serving bowl and place on the fruit plate. Put the marshmallows in another small bowl. Serve with forks or long wooden skewers for dipping—but be careful not to skewer your tongue! Eat immediately.

chopping fruit

apples

Wash and dry the apple. Peel it using a vegetable peeler. Put the apple on the chopping board so that the stem is at the top. Hold it firmly and chop it in half. Put the cut side down flat on the board and cut it in half again, do the same with the other half of the apple so you have 4 quarters. Use a knife to cut out the core by making a v-shaped cut. If you have an apple corer you could core the apple after you have peeled it and before you cut it into quarters. Ⓐ For apple slices, hold the apple quarter carefully in one hand and cut into thin slices, keeping your fingers away from the knife. Once you have your pieces of apple, you need to work carefully but quickly because the apple will start to turn brown as soon as it is cut. To help stop this, you can put the cut slices in a bowl with the juice of half a lemon, and mix them around as you add more apple.

bananas

Bananas are easy to chop because they are so soft. Peel the banana, remove the little black bits from each end, and pull off any stringy bits. Lay the banana on a chopping board and chop. If you are putting the banana in a sundae, chop it with your knife held at an angle so you have pretty slices.

mangoes

Mangoes have a thick tough skin, so make sure you have a sharp knife. They have a large flat pit in the middle, so you need to cut either side of it to get as much flesh from the fruit as possible. Put the mango on a chopping board with the thinner stem end at the top. Make a cut into the mango so that the knife is slicing downwards along the flat edge of the pit. Then cut down the other side of the pit – you should have two big boat-shaped pieces of mango. Cut them in half and then peel away the skin. If the mango is really ripe. you may be able to scoop the flesh away from the skin with a spoon. Cut as much of the flesh away from the pit as you can, and peel off any skin.

pineapples

Lie the fruit on its side on a chopping board and, using a serrated knife, slice off the top and bottom. Ⓑ Stand the fruit up on one end, hold the top in one hand and hold the knife in the other. Following the curve of the fruit, cut away a thin section of the skin. Turn the fruit slightly and cut away another strip. Continue until you have peeled the pineapple all the way around. If there are any eyes left (the little brown bits), carefully chop them out with a small sharp knife. Cut the fruit into pieces.

baking fruit

Baking is a great way to cook fruit, especially in winter when you want a dessert that will warm up your tummy!

baked apples

SERVES 4

These would be delicious served with custard sauce, vanilla ice cream, or cream.

YOU WILL NEED:

INGREDIENTS
- a little butter, for greasing
- 4 medium cooking apples, such as McIntosh or Rome
- 4 tablespoons light brown sugar
- 3 heaped tablespoons softened
- pinch of cinnamon (optional)

EQUIPMENT
- ovenproof dish
- apple corer
- small bowl
- knife
- teaspoon
- oven gloves
- aluminium foil

1 Turn the oven on to 375°F.

2 Lightly butter an ovenproof dish.

3 Wash the apples and cut the cores out using an apple corer. In a bowl, mix together the sugar, raisins, butter, and cinnamon, if you are using it.

4 Using a sharp knife score around the middle of the each apple—this will prevent them from splitting and exploding in the oven.

5 Ⓐ Use a teaspoon and your finger to push as much of the sugar mixture into the middle of each apple as possible. If there is any left over, just put it on the top of the apples since this will make a lovely sauce.

6 Put the apples into the buttered dish and using your oven gloves put them into the oven and bake 20 minutes. Using your oven gloves take them out of the oven and cover with kitchen foil. Return them to the oven and cook another 20 minutes.

OTHER GOOD FRUIT TO BAKE
- ✔ baked bananas are delicious—see recipe page 120
- ✔ baked plums or apricots—cut the fruit in half, remove the pits and lay them in a buttered ovenproof dish. Sprinkle over some brown sugar and chopped almonds or hazelnuts. Dot each half with a tiny bit of butter and bake 15–20 minutes depending on the ripeness of the fruit
- ✔ baked figs—put 6 large ripe figs into a small lightly buttered ovenproof dish. Drizzle over 3 tablespoons of runny honey and 1 tablespoon of water. Bake 20 minutes. These would be delicious served with thick Greek yogurt
- ✔ baked peaches or nectarines—cut the fruit in half and remove the pits. Put them cut side up in a lightly buttered ovenproof dish. Sprinkle over a little sugar, or vanilla sugar if you have any, and baker 10–15 minutes. Serve them warm with cream or yogurt.

baking fruit

baked bananas with easy toffee sauce

SERVES 4

People often think that bananas with black spots on them are starting to go bad, but really a banana with a sprinkling of black is exactly what a ripe banana looks like! You can try a taste test between a green banana and a spotty one—I promise the spotty one will have much more flavor and will be perfect for baking. If there is any sauce left over, it will keep well in a screw-top jar in the refrigerator for a few days. It is also lovely with baked apples or vanilla ice cream. The bananas are also really good served with some custard sauce or cream.

YOU WILL NEED:

INGREDIENTS
- butter, for greasing
- 4 large ripe bananas
- 1 tablespoon unsalted butter
- 1 tablespoon light brown sugar
- pinch of cinnamon
- juice of ½ lemon

for the toffee sauce:
- ¾ cup dark brown sugar
- 1 cup heavy cream

EQUIPMENT
- small saucepan
- wooden spoon
- pitcher
- ovenproof dish
- chopping board
- knife
- kitchen foil and oven gloves

1 Turn the oven on to 350°F.

2 Make the toffee sauce first. Put the sugar and cream in a saucepan and heat gently, stirring constantly with a wooden spoon until the sugar has dissolved. Bring the sauce to a boil and boil 5 minutes, stirring occasionally to prevent sticking. Leave the sauce to cool for a few minutes then pour into a pitcher.

3 Lightly butter an ovenproof dish. Peel the bananas and put them on a chopping board. Cut them in half lengthwise then lay them in the dish. Cut the butter into tiny pieces and dot over the bananas. Sprinkle over the sugar, cinnamon, and lemon juice.

4 Cover the dish with foil and using your oven gloves put it into the oven. Bake the bananas for 30 minutes.

5 Remove it from the oven using oven gloves. Serve the hot bananas with the toffee sauce.

lemonade

homemade pink lemonade with watermelon ice cubes

MAKES APPROX. 2 SERVINGS

This is perfect for a hot summer's day and would be just as delicious and zingy made with limes instead of lemons—because limes are smaller use 8.

YOU WILL NEED:

INGREDIENTS
- 1 large slice of watermelon—about ¾ lb
- 6 large lemons
- 1 cup superfine sugar
- 1½ teaspoons pink food coloring
- a few mint leaves

EQUIPMENT
- baking sheet
- plastic wrap
- knife
- chopping board
- lemon zester or vegetable peeler
- measuring cup
- lemon juicer
- long-handled wooden spoon
- large serving pitchers
- strainer—a conical one would be best

1 Cover the baking sheet with a piece of plastic wrap.

2 Using a knife cut the rind away from the melon and remove as many of the seeds as you can. Cut the melon into ice cube-size pieces.

3 Put the pieces of melon on to the baking sheet and put in the freezer. Leave to harden for at least 3 hours.

4 While the melon is freezing, make the lemonade. Use a vegetable peeler or lemon zester to remove as much of the lemon zest as possible, with as little of the white pith as you can.

5 Put the zest into a large measuring cup. Cut the lemons in half and use a juicer to squeeze out all the juice—don't worry if there are pits in it. Add the juice, pits, and bits to the measuring cup.

6 Bring a large saucepan of water to a boil and carefully pour out 2 ⅓ cups water into the measuring cup with the lemons.  Add the sugar and food coloring. Stir well with a wooden spoon until the sugar has dissolved.

7 Cover the measuring cup with plastic wrap and leave the lemonade to cool completely, then put into the refrigerator until the ice cubes are ready.  Put the ice cubes and the mint into a large serving pitcher. Rest a strainer over the pitcher and pour the chilled lemonade into it. Serve immediately in tall glasses.

risotto

There are many different types of risotto rice; Arborio, Carnaroli, and Vialone Nano are among the best. Risotto rice should never be washed, because it is the starch on the outside of the rice that produces the creaminess of a good risotto. When cooked properly, the rice should have a slightly firm texture. Italians call this "*al dente*."

Parmesan and herb risotto

SERVES 4

You can add other ingredients to this risotto, so long as they can cook within 20 minutes while the rice is cooking. Try adding little pieces of butternut squash, mushrooms, zucchini, peas, tomatoes, leeks, or asparagus. You could also add soft cheese, such as mozzarella, goat cheese, or soft blue cheese, just before serving the risotto. Also try other herbs, such as chopped rosemary or basil.

YOU WILL NEED:

INGREDIENTS
- ½ stick butter
- 1 onion, peeled and finely chopped
- 1 garlic clove, peeled and crushed
- 5 cups chicken or vegetable stock
- 1 ½ cups risotto rice, such as Arborio
- ¼ cup grated Parmesan
- 2 tablespoons chopped fresh parsley

EQUIPMENT
- chopping board and knife
- garlic press
- cheese grater
- 1 large saucepan
- wooden spoon
- 1 medium saucepan
- ladle
- teaspoon

1 Melt the butter in a large saucepan over a gentle heat. Add the onion and sauté gently, stirring often with a wooden spoon 10 minutes until soft.

2 Add the garlic and cook 3 minutes. Put the stock into a medium saucepan and bring up to a boil. Lower the heat and keep at a gentle simmer. **A** Add the rice to the onions and garlic and cook for 1 minute, stirring well so that all the rice grains are coated in butter.

3 **B** Pour a ladleful of hot stock over the rice. Stir well and let the mixture bubble gently. As soon as the stock is absorbed, add another ladleful and stir well. Continue to add the stock in this way, stirring often, until the mixture is creamy and the rice is cooked. This will take 20–25 minutes. Test it by putting a little on a teaspoon and blowing on it to cool it down. The rice is cooked when the middle is no longer chalky but the grain still has a bite.

4 Add a final spoonful of stock. Take the pan off the heat and using the wooden spoon, beat in the grated Parmesan. Cover the pan with a lid and leave the rice to settle for a few minutes. Take the lid off, stir in the parsley, and serve immediately.

cooking pasta

When you are cooking pasta, it is really important that you use the largest pan you can find so that the pasta does not stick together during cooking. Pasta is made without salt, so add a little salt to your pasta water.

easy tomato pasta

SERVES 4

YOU WILL NEED:
INGREDIENTS
- 2 tablespoons olive oil
- 1 red onion, peeled and finely chopped
- 2 heaped teaspoon fennel seeds
- 2 garlic cloves, peeled and sliced
- salt
- 4 good-quality pork sausages— approx. 10 oz)
- ½ cup vegetable stock or red wine
- 3 cups canned plum tomatoes, drained and chopped
- sprig of rosemary
- ¾ lb penne
- ½ cup grated Parmesan, grated

EQUIPMENT
- chopping board
- knife
- cheese grater
- heavy-based saucepan
- slotted spoon
- plate
- pestle and mortar or garlic press
- kitchen scissors
- 2 wooden spoons
- large saucepan
- timer or watch
- fork
- oven gloves
- colander

1 To make the sauce, heat half the oil in a pan and fry the onion for 5 minutes, or until soft. Using a slotted spoon, transfer it to a plate. Using a pestle and mortar, crush the fennel seeds and garlic with a pinch of salt. (Or you can crush the garlic in a garlic press and chop the seeds with a knife.)

2 Using scissors, snip the sausage skin and peel the sausages. Heat the remaining oil in the pan and add the sausage meat. Cook until well browned, stirring often with a wooden spoon to break up any big bits. Add the garlic and fennel seeds and cook for 1 minute.

3 Pour in the stock or wine, let it sizzle, and then cook it for 1 minute, stirring often to get any brown bits loose from the bottom of the pan. Add the tomatoes, cooked onions, and a sprig of rosemary and stir well. Simmer gently 10 minutes until the sauce has thickened.

4 To cook the pasta, three-quarters fill a large saucepan with water. Ideally, you need at least 4 ¾ pints of water for every ½ lb of pasta. Add a large pinch of salt, cover with a lid, and bring to a fierce boil. Carefully, but quickly, put the pasta into the pan, and use a wooden spoon to give it a good stir. If you are cooking long pasta, such as spaghetti, you will need to use the wooden spoon to push it down into the pan until it collapses into the water. Once the pasta is in the pan, the water should quickly come back to a boil.

5 Set the timer following the package instructions: Fresh pasta will take between 1–4 minutes to cook, depending on its thickness and how fresh it is; dried pasta will take 8–15 minutes to cook. You do not need to put a lid on the pan—if you cover the pasta the water will boil over.

6 Test to see if the pasta is cooked—use a fork to carefully take a piece out of the pan. Remember it will be very hot; leave it to cool slightly and then taste. If it seems too hard, cook it for another minute. Keep trying until it is cooked but still has a nice bite to it.

7 When the pasta is cooked, use your oven gloves to take the pan to the sink and drain it in a colander. Since the pan may be heavy, you might want to ask an adult for help with this. Drain and use the pasta quickly— if pasta cools it tends to go sticky and gluey. Tip the pasta back into the pan and pour over the sausage sauce. Mix well then spoon into pasta dishes. Sprinkle each serving with grated Parmesan and serve immediately.

bread dough

No-yeast breads can be very quick to make because they do not need any kneading or rising time. Instead of using yeast, this type of bread uses a rising agent, such as baking powder. When this agent is mixed with wet ingredients, such as milk and yogurt, it immediately starts to release gas bubbles, which help give the bread a light texture. It is for this reason that you mix the wet and dry ingredients separately first and then stir everything together just before you bake the bread.

no-yeast bread with nuts and seeds

MAKES A 1 LB LOAF

YOU WILL NEED:
INGREDIENTS
- 2 tablespoons canola oil
- 3 ½ cups flour, plus extra for dusting the work surface
- ¾ cup wholewheat flour
- 1 teaspoon coarse salt
- 1 level teaspoon cream of tartar
- 1 level teaspooon bicarbonate of soda
- 1 level teaspoon baking powder
- 1 cup nuts, toasted and finely chopped
- 1 cup sunflower seeds
- 100g (3½ oz) dried apricots, finely chopped
- 1 cup plain yogurt
- 2 tablespoons milk
- 1 tablespoon honey
- extra sunflower seeds, for sprinkling (optional)

EQUIPMENT
- chopping board and knife
- 2 pond loaf pan
- paper towels
- flour sifter
- wooden spoon
- pitcher
- oven gloves
- kitchen foil
- palette knife
- wire rack

1 Turn the oven on to 350°F.

2 Grease a loaf pan with half the canola oil.

3 Sift the flours, salt, cream of tartar, bicarbonate of soda, and baking powder together into a large bowl.

4 Stir in the nuts, sunflower seeds, and apricots using a wooden spoon.

5 In a pitcher mix together the yogurt, milk, honey, and remaining canola oil. Lightly flour the work-surface.

6 Pour this mixture into the dry ingredients and use the wooden spoon to mix it together until you can't see any more yogurt. Wash your hands and use one of them to mix the wet dough until it starts to come together into a ball. Tip it out on to the work surface and knead briefly until it forms one big ball of dough. Roll it into an oval shape and put it into the prepared loaf pan.

7 Sprinkle some sunflower seeds over the top.

8 Using your oven gloves put the pan into the oven and bake 40 minutes. Have a quick peek into the oven after 20 minutes—if the bread is going too brown, cover it with kitchen foil, then cooked it for a further 20 minutes.

9 Use your oven gloves to take the pan out of the oven. Leave the bread to cool 5 minutes then tip it out of the pan—you may need a palette knife to loosen it. Leave it to cool completely on a wire rack.

using yeast

Yeast is a single-cell micro-organism of the fungus family and one of the most important things that we use in cooking because it is crucial for making bread (and beer).

A The amazing thing about yeast is that it is alive. When you buy fresh yeast kept in the refrigerator, the cold makes it inactive—it will be asleep. But with a little warmth and the addition of moisture in the form of water, it will start to multiply fast. Dried or fresh yeast is mixed into warm (not hot) water. The yeast then multiplies and gives off lots of bubbles. This is what makes bread rise and gives it a lovely flavor—in the case of beer, makes it fizzy.

Fresh yeast looks like a sort of creamy pale brown cheese. It has a "squeaky" texture and a distinctive smell, like the smell of freshly baked bread in a bakery. If it smells very strong or is slimy then don't use it. Most supermarkets sell fresh yeast from the bakery section.

Fresh yeast can be stored, tightly wrapped in the refrigerator, for up to a week, and it can even be frozen for up to a month, although frozen yeast will turn to liquid when defrosted so use it immediately. Dried yeast usually comes in an envelope and looks a bit like sand. It is used in the same way as fresh yeast and gives just as good a result. High temperatures will kill yeast so it is very important to use only warm water when you dissolve it.

B When you have mixed up the yeast and water, leave it in a warm place away from drafts to froth up. This should take about 15 minutes, but can vary according to the heat in your house. If it doesn't froth up, then don't use it. If your hands are cold, run them under some warm water and dry them well before you start kneading.

kneading

what it is: The only thing you knead in the kitchen is dough and that's usually bread dough. When dough is first mixed up—normally made up of just flour, water, and yeast—it's quite sticky, lumpy, and uneven. **C** You tip it out on to a floured work surface and you start squeezing, and stretching, and punching it! You might need to do this for a good 10 minutes. This is called "kneading."

how it works: When you cut a slice of bread, it should be soft and light on the inside. Adding yeast or other rising agent, such as baking powder, makes dough rise, but kneading it helps it to rise even more and gives it the lovely soft texture. This is how it works: The bread flour used in bread making is made from wheat and wheat contains something called "gluten." Gluten is sort of like bubblegum. At first bubblegum is hard and doesn't stretch at all. Once you start chewing and it gets soft, you can blow big bubbles filled with air quite easily. Gluten is just the same. The more you stretch and squeeze it with your hands, the smoother and more elastic it becomes and the more air bubbles your dough can hold.

what to use it for: There are lots of different types of breads, both sweet and savory. Did you know that doughnuts are just fried dough? While some doughs, such as bread, need quite a thorough kneading, there are others, such as biscuits, that need just a quick, light knead. This is because you use ordinary flour, which doesn't have quite as much gluten.

using yeast

white bread

MAKES 2 X 1 LB LOAVES

You can buy fresh yeast from the bakery counter at most supermarkets. It's not usually on display so just ask, or try at your local bakery.

YOU WILL NEED:
INGREDIENTS
- small knob of butter, for greasing
- 1 pint (not hot) water
- 1 teaspoon superfine sugar
- ¾ oz fresh yeast or dried yeast
- 7 cups unbleached white bread flour, plus extra for kneading and dusting
- 1½ teaspoons salt
- ½ stick cold butter
- currants (optional)

EQUIPMENT
- 2 x 1 lb loaf pans
- pitcher
- 2 wooden spoons
- large bowl
- plastic wrap and oven gloves
- wire rack
- 2 baking sheets and kitchen scissors

OTHER GOOD THINGS TO ADD TO THIS BASIC RECIPE
- ✔ for cheese bread, add ½ lb of coarsely grated Cheddar
- ✔ for herb bread, add 4 tablespoons of chopped fresh herbs, e.g. basil
- ✔ for banana bread, add 1 large mashed banana
- ✔ for nut bread, add 1 cup of chopped toasted nuts or seeds
- ✔ for tomato bread, add ½ cup of finely chopped sun-blushed or sun-dried tomatoes
- ✔ for fruit bread, add ½ cup of chopped dried fruit, such as apricots, dates or raisins

1 Grease the loaf pans with a little butter. Put the warm water in a pitcher. Dip your finger into it; it should feel the same temperature as your finger.

2 Stir the sugar into the water, then crumble in the yeast and stir well. Leave to stand in a warm place 5 minutes; it should start to froth on the top.

3 Put the flour and salt into a large bowl and mix. Rub in the butter, then make a well in the center. Pour in the yeast mixture and mix to a dough, starting off using a wooden spoon, then using your hands in the final stages.

4 Cover with plastic wrap and leave to rise in a warm place until the dough has doubled in size—this will take 1½–2 hours. Take the dough out of the bowl and punch all the air out of it, then knead it again 5 minutes.

5 Cut the dough in half and shape each piece into an oblong with a smooth top. Drop into the pans and dust the tops with extra flour. Cover with plastic wrap and leave in a warm place until the dough rises above the sides of the pans—this will take about 30 minutes. Turn the oven on to 450°F.

6 Remove the plastic wrap and use oven gloves to put the bread into the oven 35–40 minutes until risen and golden. Use oven gloves to take it out of the oven and tip it out of the pan. Tap the bottom of the bread—it should sound hollow. If not, use oven gloves to put the bread back in the oven and bake a few more minutes.

7 When it is done, take both loaves out of their pans and cook upside down in the oven 5 minutes—this will insure a crisp crust. Cool on a wire rack.

8 To make rolls, follow the above steps up to the end of 4, greasing 2 baking sheets instead of 2 loaf pans. Divide the dough into 16 even size pieces. Roll them into smooth balls or shapes. To make a snake, roll a ball of dough into a sausage shape, then twist it up like a coiled snake, and stick 2 currants on the end for eyes. To make a porcupine, roll the dough into a ball, then pinch one end for a face, and stick in 2 currants for eyes. Use kitchen scissors to snip all over the porcupine to make spikes. Put the rolls on to the baking sheets, leaving space between them so they can rise without touching. Leave them to rise 25 minutes, then bake in the hot oven 15–20 minutes, until risen and golden (the exact time will depend on how big your rolls are).

pizza dough

Traditionally, pizza dough is made using yeast, and often, fine semolina flour. All-purpose flour works well, but the crust is not so crisp. These pizzas have a great flavor and are quick and easy to make.

super easy pizzas

MAKES 4 SMALL PIZZAS

YOU WILL NEED:

INGREDIENTS
- small knob of butter, for greasing
- 2 cups self-rising flour, plus a little extra for the work-surface
- 1½ cup milk
- ¼ cup olive oil
- 4 tablespoons tomato passata
- 2 medium mushrooms, finely sliced
- 1 slice of ham, finely chopped
- ½ cup grated Cheddar

EQUIPMENT
- chopping board, knife and grater
- baking sheet and flour sifter
- large bowl
- fork, tablespoon and oven gloves

OTHER GOOD THINGS TO PUT ON PIZZA

If you don't really like ham or are a vegetarian, don't worry. There are loads of other yummy things you can put on your pizza. Try adding:

✔ pesto and slices of mozzarella
✔ different types of sliced mushrooms and olives
✔ pepperoni or salami with some sliced red bell pepper
✔ jam or chocolate spread for a sweet pizza
✔ apple sauce and top with fruit of your choice, such as raspberries, sliced bananas, or thinly sliced apples. Sprinkle the pizzas with confectioners' sugar when you remove them from the oven

1 Turn the oven on to 350°F. Lightly grease a baking sheet by rubbing it with butter.

2 Sift the flour into a bowl and make a well in the center. Pour in the milk and olive oil and use a fork to mix it together to form a dough.

3 Lightly flour your work surface and scrape the dough out on to it using your hands. Knead it very lightly for a moment so that it is smooth and then divide it into 4 pieces.

4 Use your hands to roll each piece into a ball. Take one ball and pat it flat then use your fingers to gently pull it out into a flat round pizza shape about 4 inches in diameter. Repeat with the remaining balls of dough.

5 Lay the circles of dough on to the baking sheet.

6 **A** Use a spoon to spread 1 tablespoon of the tomato passata on to each circle. **B** Top each pizza with mushrooms and ham then sprinkle over the grated cheese.

7 Use your oven gloves to put the tray in the oven. Bake 8–10 minutes, until golden. Use the oven gloves to take the tray out of the oven, let the pizzas cool a little but eat them while they are still warm.

biscuit dough

Biscuit dough is very versatile and you can easily adapt it. If you prefer something fruity or savory, just have a look at the suggestions below.

biscuit magic

MAKES 8

This recipe is for sweet biscuits traditionally served with butter and jam.

YOU WILL NEED:

INGREDIENTS
- small knob of butter, for greasing
- 2 cups all-purpose flour, plus extra for kneading
- 2 level teaspoons baking powder
- 4½ stick chilled butter, cut into cubes
- 1½ tablespoons golden caster sugar
- pinch of salt
- ⅔ cup milk, plus a little extra
- jam and butter

EQUIPMENT
- baking sheet
- flour sifter and large bowl
- knife
- round cutter approx. 2½ inches
- pastry brush
- oven gloves and wire rack

OTHER GOOD THINGS TO ADD TO BISCUITS

✔ for fruit BISCUITS add 50 g (1¾ oz) of dried fruit, such as raisins, currants or sultanas, or chopped dried apricots or apple. Just stir it in when you add the sugar. Try adding a pinch of mixed spice or cinnamon

✔ for cheesy BISCUITS leave out the sugar out and stir in 50g (1¾ oz) of grated Cheddar. You could also add some chopped fresh herbs

1 Turn the oven on to 425°F. Rub a baking sheet with a little butter.

2 Sift the flour and baking powder into a large bowl.

3 Rub in the butter using your fingertips—when it is done the mixture should look like fine breadcrumbs. Stir in the sugar and salt.

4 Use an ordinary knife to mix in the milk, a little at a time, until the mixture starts to come together.

5 Sprinkle a little flour on to your work surface, then tip the dough out of the bowl. Put a little flour on your hands and very lightly knead the mixture half a minute until it is smooth.

6 Form the mixture into a ball and use your hands to lightly pat it out to about 1¼ inches thick. Dip a round cutter into a little flour and cut out biscuits from the dough. Put the biscuits on to the baking tray, spaced a little apart.

7 Gather all the spare bits of dough together and roll together to make a ball and flatten it out again. Cut out the rest of the biscuits—you should be able to make 8. Brush the tops of the biscuits with a little milk.

8 Using your oven gloves put the biscuits into the oven and bake 8–10 minutes until risen and golden. Then use your oven gloves to remove the baking sheet from the oven. Cool the biscuits on a wire rack then eat them with jam and butter.

how flour is made

Cereals come from grasses that used to grow wild. Thousands of years ago, humans started to farm crops such as wheat, corn, rice, oats, barley, and rye. Grains from these cereals can be eaten whole or they can be ground up.

The grains of the cereal, for example, wheat grains, can be ground really fine until they look like powder. This is called flour. People made flour hundreds of years ago by grinding the grains between stones. This took a long time and the flour was quite rough, making the bread quite heavy. Later on, people used animals, wind, and water power to help them grind bigger stones together. They did this by building mills. These could be simple stones in a field, or a watermill, or windmill. Inside these mills are big, heavy stones which are slowly turned to grind large quantities of grain down into flour. This method was much easier, although it was still quite slow. During the Industrial Revolution people used steel rollers to make flour. This was much faster, but a lot of the flavor and nutrients were lost. Stoneground flours are widely available today.

Flour is a key ingredient in all types of baking. The main type of flour used in cooking today is made from wheat. The wheat kernel consists of three parts: bran, germ, and endosperm. The wheat bran is the husk that surrounds the kernel and the nutritious wheat germ is the seed that makes another plant. The middle part of the kernel, the endosperm, is full of starch and protein. Wheat is divided into different types according to the hardness of the grain. This hardness refers to the protein content of the wheat kernels. If the wheat has a high protein content, it is perfect for breadmaking. When you knead dough to make bread, the protein in the flour develops into gluten—an elastic substance.

types of flour
Wholewheat flour is made from the complete wheat kernel, with nothing removed, so it looks brown and has a coarse texture and nutty taste. If you use wholewheat flour on its own to make bread, the bread will have a full flavor, but it may have a dense texture because the bran stops the bread from rising too much. For the perfect loaf you could try mixing this flour with some white bread flour.

All-purpose flour is the most commonly used flour in bread and cake making, because it has many different uses. It is made from a blend of hard and soft wheat and can be used for pastries, cookies, and batter.

White bread flour is milled from hard wheat that has more protein in it than the wheat used to make all-purpose flour.

Self-rising flour is all-purpose flour with a rising agent, such as baking powder, added to it.

Cake flour contains the least gluten.

Coarse semolina flour is made from one of the hardest varieties of wheat—durum wheat. It can be mixed with all-purpose flour to make bread.

Fine semolina is also made from the endosperm of durum wheat, but it is ground twice to produce a fine flour that is ideal for breadmaking.

Brown flour contains most of the wheat grain's germ but has had some of the bran removed. A loaf made with this flour will have a lighter texture than a loaf made with wholewheat flour.

You can also buy flours made from cereals other than wheat—for example, rye, oats, barley, and corn. The seeds vary in size and shape, but they are all similar to the wheat kernel. Ground dried corn kernels, called polenta, are a staple food in parts of Italy. The Italians eat polenta with their meat or fish. Rye flour is made from ground rye grains. You only need to add a little of this flour to other flour to give bread a distinctive flavor.

Once you have mastered the bread recipe (see page 128), try experimenting with different flours to see what you think of their different tastes and textures.

sponge cake

Superfine sugar is the best sugar for making cakes because the grains are very small, unlike granulated sugar which can give a slightly speckled effect when the cake is baked. Confectioners' sugar, on the other hand, is too fine. Make sure your eggs are at room temperature. If they are too cold, the cake mixture may curdle. I use self-rising flour so that I do not need to add baking powder.

sponge cake special

SERVES 8

YOU WILL NEED:

INGREDIENTS
- 2 sticks butter, softened plus a little extra for greasing
- 1 cup superfine sugar
- 4 large eggs
- 1–2 drops vanilla extract
- 2 ¼ cups cake flour
- 2 teaspoons baking powder
- 4 tablespoons raspberry jam
- 2 tablespoons confectioners' sugar, for sprinkling

for the buttercream (optional):
- 2 sticks butter, softened
- ½ lb cream cheese
- 1 cup confectioners' sugar
- 1–2 drops of pink food coloring
- M&M's (optional)

EQUIPMENT
- 2 x 8 inch layer cake pans
- baking parchment
- pencil
- kitchen scissors
- large bowl
- wooden spoon
- fork
- tablespoon
- flour sifter
- large metal spoon
- oven gloves, wire rack
- palette knife

1 Turn the oven on to 350°F. Rub the cake pans with a little butter. Rest one of the pans on a piece of baking parchment and draw around the pan with a pencil. Cut the circle out and put the paper inside the pan. Do the same for the second pan.

2 Put the softened butter and sugar into a large bowl and, using a wooden spoon, beat them together. As the mixture is beaten it will become fluffy and nearly white in color. Put the eggs into a small bowl and, using a fork, beat them together. Add a tablespoon at a time of the eggs to the butter and sugar, beating really well after each addition. Beat in the vanilla.

3 Sift the flour and baking powder over the butter mixture and, using a large metal spoon, fold the flour in gently. To fold, hold the spoon over the middle of the bowl and cut through the middle of the mixture, then move the spoon across the bottom of the bowl and up the other side. The idea is to fold in the flour quickly and gently so you don't lose any air from the mixture.

4 Spoon the mixture into the prepared pans. Using your oven gloves, put the cakes into the oven and bake 15 minutes, or until the cakes are well risen and cooked through. Try not to open the oven door until just a couple of minutes before the end of the cooking time. Using your oven gloves, take the cakes out of the oven and gently touch the center of the cake. If it is cooked it will feel firm and springy. If your finger makes an indentation that does not spring back you will need to bake the cake another 2–3 minutes and then check again. The cake will also start to pull away slightly from the edges of the pan if it is cooked.

5 Rest the cake pans on a wire rack and leave to cool slightly, then turn the cakes out of the pans, peel the paper away, and leave on the wire rack to cool. When the cakes are cool, spread the jam on to the bottom of one of the cakes, then rest the other cake on top so that the smooth side is facing uppermost. Sprinkle the top with confectioners' sugar.

6 If you want to use buttercream instead of jam and sugar, put the butter and cream cheese in a bowl and beat with a wooden spoon until soft and smooth. Sift the confectioners' sugar into the bowl and mix gently. When the sugar is mixed in, add the food coloring and beat until the color is even. Use a palette knife dipped in warm water to spread half of the buttercream in the middle of the cake and the rest on the top. Decorate with M&M's.

sponge cake

flower cakes

MAKES 12 LARGE CUPCAKES

There are so many ways that you can decorate cupcakes, but these cakes look particularly pretty and are very easy to do.

YOU WILL NEED:

INGREDIENTS

- 1½ sticks unsalted butter, softened
- 1¾ cups superfine sugar
- 3 large eggs, beaten
- 1½ cups cake flour
- 2 teaspoons baking powder
- 2 tablespoons milk

for the frosting:
- 1½ cups confectioners' sugar
- hot water
- 1–2 drops of pink food coloring
- M&M's

EQUIPMENT

- 10–12 paper cupcake cups
- 12-hole muffin pan
- large bowl
- electric mixer
- 2 wooden spoons
- flour sifter
- metal spoon
- oven gloves
- wire rack
- small bowl
- teaspoon

1 Turn the oven on to 350°F.

2 Put the paper cupcake cups into the holes of the muffin pan. Put the butter and sugar into a large bowl and beat together using an electric mixer or wooden spoon until the mixture is pale and fluffy.

3 (A) Add a little of the beaten egg and beat well, then add a little more and beat again. Continue like this until all the egg is used up.

4 (B) Sift the flour into this mixture and gently mix it in using a metal spoon. Then stir in the milk so that the mixture softens enough to drop easily from the spoon—this is called "dropping consistency."

5 Spoon the mixture into the paper cups, to come about three-quarters of the way up. Using oven gloves, put the pan into the oven and baker 15–20 minutes until risen and golden and the cakes are springy to touch.

6 Using oven gloves, take the pan out of the oven and let the cakes cool for a minute, then lift them out on to a wire rack and leave to cool completely.

7 For the frosting, sift the confectioners' sugar into a bowl and mix in a little hot water until you have a thick pouring consistency. Add the food coloring and mix.

8 Pour teaspoons of the frosting on to the cakes and decorate with M&M's to make flower shapes. Leave to set, then store in an airtight container if you're not eating them immediately.

sponge cake

gooey chocolate birthday cake

SERVES 8–10

This is a really moist and delicious chocolate cake—perfect for special occasions such as birthdays.

YOU WILL NEED:
INGREDIENTS
- butter, for greasing
- 1⅔ cups cake flour
- 1½ level teaspoons baking powder
- 2 cups hot cocoa mix
- 1½ sticks butter, softened
- ¾ cup light brown sugar
- 4 large eggs

for the chocolate frosting:
- ½ lb milk chocolate (at least 40% cocoa)
- 2 oz good-quality bittersweet chocolate (at least 70% cocoa)
- 2 cups heavy cream
- ½ teaspoon vanilla extract
- M&M's or strawberries, to decorate

EQUIPMENT
- 2 x 8 inch layer cake pans
- baking parchment
- pencil
- kitchen scissors
- flour sifter
- 2 large bowls
- hand electric mixer
- spoon
- spatula
- oven gloves
- medium bowl
- small saucepan
- small wooden spoon
- wire rack
- serving plate
- palette knife
- birthday candles (optional)

1　Turn the oven on to 350°F.

2　Rub the base and sides of the cake pans with a small piece of butter. Line the base of each with a piece of baking parchment (see page 137, point 1, for how to line a cake pan).

3　Sift the flour, baking powder, and cocoa mix into a large bowl.

4　Put the butter in another bowl and beat with the electric mixer. Gradually add the sugar, continuing to beat until the mixture is pale and fluffy.

5　Add 1 of the eggs to the butter mixture and beat well, then add a spoonful of the flour mixture and beat again. Continue to add eggs and flour alternately, beating well between each addition. Continue until you have used everything up.

6　Divide the mixture between the 2 prepared pains, using the spatula to scrape the mixture out of the bowl. Smooth the tops of the mixture, making sure it is spread out evenly. Use your oven gloves to put the pans into the oven and bake 25 minutes.

7　Now make the frosting. Break the chocolate into pieces into a medium bowl. Half fill a saucepan with water and set over a medium heat. Rest the bowl on top and let the chocolate melt, stirring until it is smooth. Remove from the heat and let cool for a few minutes. Add the cream and vanilla, stirring all the time until you have a thick smooth frosting.

8　Use your oven gloves to remove the pans from the oven and leave the cakes to cool for 15 minutes. Turn the cakes upside down on to the wire rack and peel off the baking parchment. Put one of the cakes on to a serving plate. Put a third of the frosting into the middle of the cake and spread it evenly to the edges using the palette knife.

9　Rest the second cake on top. Put half of the remaining icing on top of the cake and spread it evenly to the edges. Spread the rest of the icing around the sides of the cake. Decorate the cake with M&M's or strawberries any way you want. Make them into a number and add birthday candles if it is someone's birthday!

teabread

Teabreads are quite plain cakes made in the shape of a loaf. They originated in the countryside, where they were part of an early supper, eaten at the end of the day in winter or before a last stint of work in summer. They tend to be made with similar ingredients to cakes.

Caribbean banana teabread

MAKES 1 LOAF

Bananas help to keep this cake really moist. If there is any left over it often tastes better the next day. This is best made in a loaf pan. If you can find a loaf pan liner—available from most kitchenware stores—then use that. This will help to keep the loaf moist. If you don't have one, just grease the pan really well and line the base with baking parchment.

YOU WILL NEED:

INGREDIENTS
- butter, for greasing (optional)
- 3–4 very ripe bananas—ones with black spots on them are best
- 1 stick butter, softened
- ½ cup light brown sugar
- 2 large eggs
- 2 ½ cups all-purpose flour
- 3 teaspoons baking powder
- pinch of cinnamon
- ⅔ cup chopped walnuts or small chunks of milk chocolate

EQUIPMENT
- chopping board
- knife
- 2 lb loaf pan
- loaf pan liner or baking parchment
- plate
- fork
- large bowl
- wooden spoon or electric mixer
- flour sifter
- spatula
- oven gloves
- skewer
- wire rack

1 Turn the oven on to 375°F. Line the loaf pan with a loaf pan liner or butter it well and then line the bottom with baking parchment (see page 137, point 1).

2 Put the bananas on a plate and mash with a fork until there are no more big lumps.

3 Put the butter and sugar into a large bowl and beat together until soft and smooth. You can use a wooden spoon or an electric mixer to do this.

4 Beat in the eggs.

5 Sift the flour and cinnamon into the bowl and mix in. Add the bananas and walnuts or chocolate chunks and mix it all together.

6 Spoon the mixture into the prepared pan, using a spatula to scrape the mixture out of the bowl.

7 Using oven gloves put the pan into the oven and bake 50 minutes until risen and golden and a skewer inserted in the loaf comes out clean.

8 Using your oven gloves again, remove the pan from the oven. Leave the pan to cool 15 minutes on a wire rack then turn out the loaf and peel off the baking parchment. Eat immediately or store in an airtight container.

shortcrust pastry

MAKES ENOUGH TO LINE A 9 INCH PIE PAN

Once you have learned how to make pastry, you can make lots of new things, but jam tarts (see opposite) are about the easiest!

YOU WILL NEED:

INGREDIENTS
- 2 ½ cups all-purpose flour, plus extra for dusting
- pinch of salt
- 1 stick cold butter
- 1–2 tablespoons very cold water

EQUIPMENT
- flour sifter
- large bowl
- table knife
- tablespoon
- plastic wrap
- rolling pin

1 Sift the flour and salt into a large mixing bowl, holding the sifter high above the bowl so the flour gets a good airing

2 Cut the cold butter into small pieces then stir it into the flour using a knife. Rub the butter into the flour by dipping your fingertips into the flour and gently rub the little pieces of butter between the tips of your thumbs and fingers so that they flatten and gradually mix into the flour. As you do this keep lifting your hands up above the rim of the bowl. This will let air get into the flour and keep the mixture cool.

3 Gently shake the bowl occasionally because this will make bits of butter come to the surface and you can rub them in. Keep rubbing in as lightly as you can until you cannot see any more bits of butter and the mixture looks like coarse breadcrumbs. Try to do the rubbing in as quickly as possible because the longer you touch the butter the hotter it will become and your mixture may become greasy and sticky. If this happens just put the bowl in the refrigerator 5 minutes and then continue.

4 Wash your hands, then run them under cold water and dry them thoroughly. (A) Sprinkle 1 tablespoon of cold water over the mixture and quickly mix it in with the knife. The pastry will start to come together in small lumps. If there are any dry bits of flour in the bottom of the bowl sprinkle over a tiny bit more water and mix again. It is very important not to add too much liquid because the pastry will become sticky and difficult to roll out, and when it is cooked the pastry will be tough and hard.

5 (B) Use your hands to bring the pastry together in a ball. This is easiest if you use a wiping motion and wipe all the little bits up into one big ball. The dough should feel like plasticine—not too hard and not too soft. Tip it out on to a floured work surface and knead it for a second or two just to bring it into a smooth ball. Wrap the pastry in a piece of plastic wrap and leave to rest in the refrigerator 30 minutes.

6 Clean up the work surface, make sure it is really dry, and sprinkle it with a little flour.

7 Take the pastry out of the refrigerator, unwrap it from the plastic wrap and set it on the floured work surface. Flour your hands and a rolling pin.

8 Pat the dough down a little so the surface is flat. Use the rolling pin to roll the pastry away from you in gentle strokes, pressing down with it gently as you go. After every two or three strokes give the pastry a quarter turn—this will ensure you have a circle of pastry instead of a long thin strip. Keep rolling until the pastry is the required thickness—generally the smaller the pan you are lining, the thinner the pastry should be.

sweet shortcrust pastry

Once you have mastered making a plain shortcrust pastry for savory dishes, such as tarts and quiches, you could try making sweet pastry. There are many variations, but one of the simplest is to add a little sugar for sweetness and an egg yolk for a rich flavor and texture. You can also change the flavor of the pastry by adding a little cocoa powder to the mixture (see page 146).

fruity jam tarts

MAKES 18

Try using different kinds of jam when you make these so you have a plateful of lovely jewel-like tarts.

YOU WILL NEED:

INGREDIENTS
- 2 ½ cups all-purpose flour, plus extra for dusting
- 1 stick chilled butter, cut into small pieces, plus a little extra for greasing
- 1 teaspoon superfine sugar
- 1 large egg yolk
- 1–2 tablespoons cold water
- 18 heaped teaspoons jam, such as raspberry, apricot, strawberry or cherry

EQUIPMENT
- flour sifter
- large bowl
- table knife
- plastic wrap
- rolling pin
- fluted cookie cutter approx. 3 inch diameter
- 2 x12 tartlet pans or 2 x 12-hole tart pans
- fork
- oven gloves
- teaspoon
- palette knife
- wire rack

1 Sift the flour into a large bowl, then add the butter, and rub it in using your fingertips until the mixture looks like coarse breadcrumbs.

2 Add the sugar and mix together. Use a knife to mix in the egg yolk, then add the water, a little at a time, stirring with the knife until the mixture comes together and you can form a ball with your hands. See opposite for a step-by-step guide to making pastry.

3 Wrap the pastry in a piece of plastic wrap and put it in the refrigerator 30 minutes—this will make it easier to roll out.

4 Turn the oven on to 400°F. Rub the tart pans with a little butter. Take the pastry out of the refrigerator and unwrap it. (A) Sprinkle your work surface and your rolling pin with a little flour and roll the pastry out to about ⅛ inch thick.

5 Dip the cutter in flour, then cut circles—you may need to gather the bits of pastry up and roll them out again to make 18. Lay a circle in each tart pan and press it into place. Prick the base of each tart once with a fork.

6 Use oven gloves to put the tart pans in the oven. Bake for 6 minutes, until the pastry is pale golden. Using oven gloves, take the pan(s) out of the oven. (B) Put 1 teaspoon of jam into each tart and, using oven gloves, put the tray back into the oven for 6 minutes. Using oven gloves, take the tray out and leave the tarts to cool for a few minutes, then use a palette knife to gently lift them out of the pan(s) to cool completely on a wire rack.

sweet shortcrust pastry

white choc and raspberry tarts

MAKES 12

A great idea for an easy, but impressive, dessert that is really good fun to make.

YOU WILL NEED:

INGREDIENTS
- 1 ¾ cups all-purpose flour, plus extra for dusting
- 3 teaspoons good quality cocoa powder
- 1 heaped tablespoon confectioners' sugar
- ¾ stick cold butter, cut into small cubes
- 1 large egg yolk
- 1 teaspoon cold water
- a little confectioners' sugar, for dusting

for the filling:
- 3½ oz good quality white chocolate
- ½ cup heavy cream
- ½ lb raspberries

EQUIPMENT
- flour sifter, large bowl
- knife
- plastic wrap
- rolling pin
- cookie cutter (4 inch) diameter
- 12-hole tart pan or 12 tartlet pans
- fork, oven gloves
- medium bowl
- medium saucepan
- small wooden spoon
- small palette knife
- spoon

1 Sift the flour, cocoa, and confectioners' sugar into a large bowl. Rub in the cold butter. Stir in the egg yolk and water until the pastry starts to come together, then use your hands to bring everything together in a ball (see page 145, points 1–2).

2 Tip it out on to a floured work surface and knead it a second or 2 just to bring it together in a smooth ball, then wrap it in plastic wrap, and leave it to rest in the refrigerator for 30 minutes.

3 Turn the oven on to 400°F. Rub the tart pan(s) with a little butter. Take the pastry out of the refrigerator and unwrap it. Sprinkle your work surface and rolling pin with a little flour and roll the pastry out to about ⅛ inch thick.

4 Cut out as many circles as you can—you may need to gather the bits of pastry up and roll them out again to make 12 circles. Lay the circles of pastry in the tart pans and press them gently into place. Prick the bases of the tarts with a fork and, using oven gloves, put them into the oven 6–8 minutes.

5 Using oven gloves, take the pan out of the oven and leave to cool.

6 Break the chocolate up into small pieces and put into a medium bowl over a pan of gently simmering water. When the chocolate has melted, leave it to cool slightly—if you dip a clean finger into it should feel the same temperature as your finger.

7 Pour the cream into the chocolate and stir until it is just mixed together.

8 Use a small palette knife to lift the tart shells out of the pan and carefully fill each one with a generous spoonful of the cream mixture. Top each one with a few fresh raspberries, dust with a little confectioners' sugar, and serve immediately.

cookies

A cookie is a small, crisp pastry, either sweet or savory, or a soft and/or chewy small cake. There are many ways to make cookies, but this recipe uses the "creaming method" of beating butter and sugar together until light to incorporate air. Eggs are then added before the flour, cocoa, and chocolate.

chocolate orange cookies

MAKES 18 COOKIES

YOU WILL NEED:

INGREDIENTS
- 3½ oz each of orange-flavored milk chocolate and white chocolate
- 1 stick butter, softened
- ½ cup light brown sugar
- 2 drops vanilla extract
- 1 medium egg
- 2 tablespoons golden or corn syrup
- 1 ⅓ cups all-purpose flour
- 1 level tablespoon baking powder
- 2 tablespoons quality cocoa powder

EQUIPMENT
- baking sheets and baking parchment
- chopping board and knife
- large bowl, wooden spoon and sifter
- oven gloves

OTHER GOOD THINGS TO ADD TO COOKIES
- ✔ toasted chopped nuts, e.g. hazelnuts, pecans, or walnuts
- ✔ dried fruit, e.g. raisins,
- ✔ different type of chocolate chunks, e.g. milk or white

1 Turn the oven on to 350°F. Line 2 baking sheets with baking parchment.

2 Put the chocolate on to a chopping board and chop it into big chunks using a knife.

3 **A** Put the butter, sugar, and vanilla into a large bowl and beat together using a wooden spoon until the mixture is pale and fluffy.

4 Add the egg and golden or corn syrup and beat for 2 more minutes.

5 Sift the flour, baking powder, and cocoa powder into the bowl and gently mix it in until the mixture is smooth. **B** Stir in the chocolate chunks.

6 Spoon walnut-sized blobs of the mixture on to the prepared baking sheets, allowing space for them to spread.

7 Use your oven gloves to put the baking sheets into the oven and cook 7 minutes. Remove the baking sheets from the oven with your oven gloves and leave to cool until the cookies are firm, then carefully peel them off the baking paper.

8 Eat immediately or store in an airtight cookie jar.

krispies

Although this isn't strictly a technique, it seemed to be impossible to write a cook book for children without including this all-time favorite. If you make these at Eastertime, make them into nests. When you have put the mixture into the shells, use a metal teaspoon to make a hollow in the middle of each krispie, like a nest. When they have set, you can rest some chocolate eggs in the hollow.

toffee marshmallow krispies

MAKES 12

YOU WILL NEED:

INGREDIENTS
- 2 ¾ oz caramels, unwrapped
- ¾ stick unsalted butter
- 1 ½ cups small marshmallows
- 1 tablespoon golden or corn syrup
- 2 ½ cups Rice Krispies

EQUIPMENT
- 12 paper cupcake cups
- 12-hole muffin pan
- large saucepan
- wooden spoon
- spatula
- metal spoon

1 Put the paper cupcake cups into the holes of the muffin pan.

2 Put the caramels, butter, marshmallows, and golden or corn syrup into a saucepan.

3 (A) Heat very gently, stirring occasionally with a wooden spoon, until everything is melted and the mixture is smooth—this will take about 3 minutes.

4 (B) Take the pan off the heat and add the Rice Krispies. Stir everything together—this is easiest using a plastic spatula so you can scrape up all the sticky liquid from the bottom of the pan.

5 Working quickly, before the mixture sets, use a metal spoon to put spoonfuls of the mixture into the paper cupcake cups until all the mixture is used up.

6 Leave the krispies to set for at least an hour. Eat immediately or store in an airtight container.

snackjacks

A snackjack should not be too sweet or sticky and similarly not too 'oaty'.

snackjacks

MAKES 15

YOU WILL NEED:

INGREDIENTS
- butter, for greasing
- ⅓ cup light soft brown sugar
- 1 ½ sticks butter
- ½ cup golden or corn syrup
- 4 cups rolled oats

EQUIPMENT
- 10 inch pan with 1 inch high sides
- large saucepan and wooden spoon
- oven gloves, knife, and wire rack

OTHER GOOD THINGS TO ADD TO SNACKJACKS
- ✔ chopped dried fruit, such as apricots or raisins
- ✔ chopped toasted nuts, such as hazelnuts or pecans
- ✔ seeds, such as sesame seeds, pumpkin seeds
- ✔ they are also good half dipped in melted chocolate—just dip them and leave them to cool on some baking parchment

1 Turn the oven on to 350°F.

2 Rub the butter lightly over the base and sides of the pan.

3 Put the sugar, butter, and golden or corn syrup into a pan. Heat gently over a low heat until the butter is melted and the sugar has dissolved, stirring often with a wooden spoon. Turn the heat up and bring the mixture to a boil. Turn the heat off immediately.

4 **A** Put the oats into the pan. Stir with the wooden spoon until there are no pockets of dry oats—they should be covered in the syrup mixture.

5 **B** Tip the mixture into the prepared pan and spread it out evenly right to the edges. Use the back of the spoon to smooth the top.

6 Using oven gloves, put the pan into the oven and bake 10–15 minutes until golden.

7 Using oven gloves, take the pan out of the oven and leave the snackjacks to cool for 5 minutes.

8 While the snackjacks are still warm, use a knife to mark them into squares. Leave to cool completely then lift them out on to a wire rack. Eat immediately or store in an airtight container.

popcorn

Popcorn is very easy to cook, but since you need to get the oil quite hot you should ask an adult to help you. A lot of people wonder how corn pops. Well, inside each hard little kernel there is some water—not much, but enough. When the corn is heated, the water turns to steam, which is a gas that needs more space than water. The only way for it to find space is to break out of the kernel by exploding, making the corn kernels pop open.

sweet popcorn

MAKES A BIG BOWLFUL

YOU WILL NEED:
INGREDIENTS
- 2 tablespoons canola oil
- 2½ oz popping corn
- 2 teaspoons superfine sugar

EQUIPMENT
- large heavy-based saucepan with lid
- wooden spoon and serving bowl

OTHER GOOD THINGS TO ADD TO POPCORN
- ✔ vanilla sugar instead of ordinary sugar
- ✔ light brown sugar for a more caramel flavor
- ✔ 1 tablespoon of corn syrup or maple syrup
- ✔ mix a pinch of cinnamon into your sugar
- ✔ for savory popcorn, try adding crunchy peanut butter (about 2 tablespoons), or ½ cup finely grated Cheddar or Parmesan

1 Put the oil into a large saucepan and heat until the oil is hot. Tip the corn into the pan, spreading it out so it covers the base of the pan.

2 Cook the corn until it starts to pop, then put on the lid immediately. (If you have a pan with a glass lid this is fun to watch.)

3 Cook the corn 2–3 more minutes. Hold the lid on tightly and shake the pan often. Keep cooking until the sound of popping corn stops.

4 Remove from the heat, take off the lid, and pour over the sugar. Stir gently with a wooden spoon and tip into a serving bowl. Eat immediately.

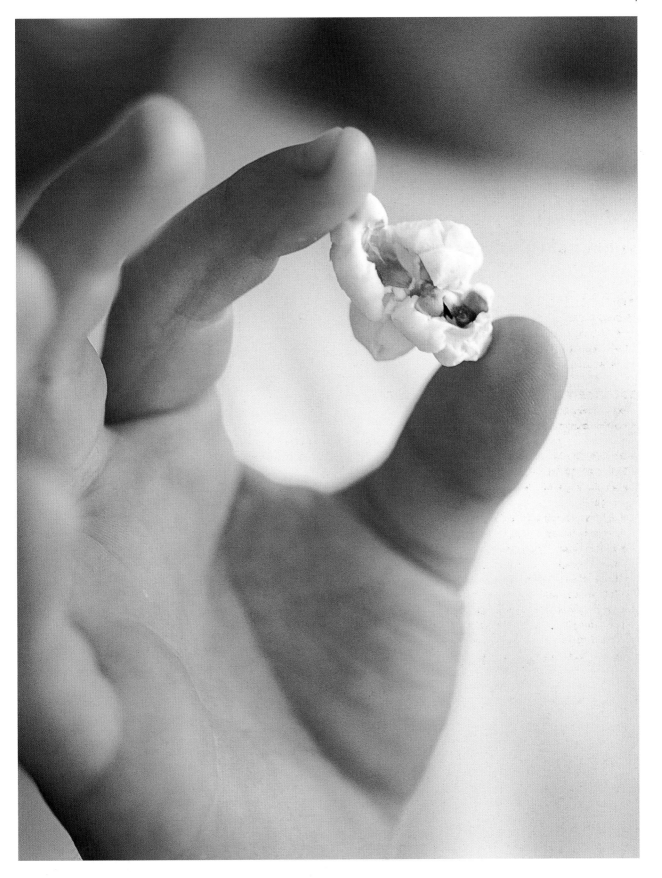

6 FROM AFAR

stir-frying vegetables

Stir-frying is a quick method of cooking used mainly for Chinese food. You will need to use a wok or a very large skillet and you must cook the food quickly over a very high heat. To make sure the food is cooked evenly you will need to keep stirring the ingredients around in the pan, which is why it is called "stir-frying."

Chinese stir-fry with cashew nuts

SERVES 4

YOU WILL NEED:
INGREDIENTS
- 1 red bell pepper
- 1 inch piece of fresh ginger
- 3 scallions, trimmed
- 1 garlic clove, peeled and crushed
- 1 small ripe pineapple
- ½ lb snow peas
- 2 tablespoons vegetable oil
- 3 teaspoons sesame oil
- ½ lb bean sprouts
- ½ cup cashew nuts
- 1 tablespoon light soy sauce
- freshly ground black pepper
- ½ lb egg thread noodles, boiled according to the package instructions

EQUIPMENT
- garlic press
- large saucepan
- colander
- chopping board
- knife
- vegetable peeler
- small bowl
- large plate
- wok or skillet
- wooden spatula

1 Using a chopping board and a knife, cut the red bell pepper in half, remove the seeds, and thinly slice the flesh.

2 Peel the ginger and finely chop it. Thinly slice the scallions. Place in a small bowl with the garlic. Put the pineapple on to a board, cut off its bottom and crown (the top part where the leaves stick out), then lay it flat-side down, and cut the skin off the flesh—see page 118. Pick out the eyes (the little round brown circles) and cut the flesh into bite-size pieces. Keep all the vegetables, including the peas, and pineapple in separate bundles on a plate.

3 Heat a wok or skillet over a high heat until very hot. Pour in the oils (see page 160, point 3). **A** Add the garlic, ginger, and scallions and stir around with a wooden spatula 1 minute.

4 **B** Cook the hardest vegetables first, so start by adding the bell pepper and snow peas and cook 1 minute. Add the pineapple chunks, bean sprouts, and cashew nuts and keep stirring for 1 minute.

5 Add the soy sauce and season with freshly ground black pepper. As soon as the vegetables are cooked, but still crunchy, add the noodles. Mix everything together and eat immediately.

stir-frying vegetables

Stir-frying is a fast method of cooking that can be used to fry meat, fish, or vegetables. The following guidelines will help to make sure that you find it both easy and successful.

to stir-fry:

1   Prepare all your ingredients before you begin cooking. All the chopping, slicing, and getting sauces ready has to be done before you start to stir-fry. Have everything laid out ready to go, a little like the way you often see it on TV. This is really important to make sure that you do not overcook or undercook any of the ingredients.

2   If you are using noodles or rice, make sure that they have been soaked and drained, or cooked, before you begin stir-frying.

3   Put the wok (or skillet) over the heat and heat until really hot before you add the oil. Once you add the oil, swirl it around the pan and then add your other ingredients immediately.

4   You will need to adjust the heat as you stir-fry—turning it up when you add more food to the wok and down a little when the food starts to cook.

5   When you become more confident with a wok and stir-frying, you can move the food that is cooked to the top part of the wok—furthest away from the heat—while the remaining ingredients cook at the bottom.

6   The first ingredients to go in the wok should be those that will take the longest to cook. For example, carrots and broccoli will take longer to cook than scallions or bean sprouts. This is worth thinking about if you are adding your own vegetables and not following a recipe.

7   Try experimenting with different ingredients in your stir-fries: Fruit, such as pineapple, and nuts, such as cashew nuts (see page 159), can add lots of flavor and texture to your finished meal.

curry paste

A curry paste is an intensely flavored mixture of herbs and spices that is used in curries and other dishes. This is a Thai red curry paste. Store in an airtight container in the refrigerator—a jam jar is ideal. Be careful when chopping chilies: Wash your hands thoroughly afterwards and don't touch your face, especially your eyes—the chili juice can really sting!

curry paste

MAKES APPROX 4 TABLESPOONS

YOU WILL NEED:
INGREDIENTS
- 6 medium red chilies
- 2 sticks of lemon grass
- 1 inch piece of fresh ginger
- 2 shallots
- 3 garlic cloves
- 1 teaspoons each of cilantro seeds, cumin seeds, and black peppercorns
- 1 teaspoon lime zest
- 1 tablespoon lime juice
- 2 tablespoons fresh cilantro

EQUIPMENT
- lemon zester
- chopping board
- knife
- tall jug
- vegetable peeler
- skillet
- hand-held blender or small food processor

1 Use a chopping board and a knife to prepare the ingredients.

2 Cut the chilies in half, scoop out the seeds, and finely chop. Put into a tall pitcher.

3 Remove the tough outer layer of the lemon grass stalks and finely chop what's left, but throw away the tough ends. Add to the chilies.

4 (A) Peel the fresh ginger and finely chop the flesh, then add to the chilies and lemon grass.

5 Peel the shallots and finely chop, and add to the other ingredients.

6 Peel the garlic and finely chop, adding to the rest.

7 (B) Put the cilantro seeds, cumin seeds, and black peppercorns into a dry skillet. Heat over a high heat until the seeds just start to pop. This dry-frying helps to bring out the flavor of the spices.

8 Add the aromatics, lime zest, and juice along with the fresh cilantro to the pitcher and use a hand blender to blend the mixture to a paste. Alternatively, put all the prepared ingredients into a small food processor and process to make a paste in the same way.

curry paste

Amanda's Thai red fish curry

SERVES 4–5

Many of the ingredients for a Thai curry, such as kaffir lime leaves and red curry paste, can be found in supermarkets now, but you'll also find good quality ingredients in many delis and Chinese/Thai supermarkets. If you can't find kaffir lime leaves, you could use some lime zest instead. Special thanks to Amanda, a wonderful friend, for sharing her curry secrets, on which this recipe is based.

YOU WILL NEED:
INGREDIENTS

- 1 lb salmon fillet, monkish, etc
- 1¼ lbs squash (you will need 3 cups peeled)
- 3 pak choi
- 1 tablespoon canola oil
- 1–2 tablespoons good quality Thai red curry paste (see page 161)
- ½ teaspoon turmeric
- 1⅔ cups coconut milk
- 1½ cups fish stock
- 3 tablespoons fish sauce, plus extra to taste
- 2 teaspoons superfine sugar
- 3–5 lemon grass stalks, bruised (hit with a rolling pin to split them open slightly)
- 6 kaffir lime leaves
- half a bunch fresh cilantro, chopped
- freshly ground black pepper
- steamed Thai jasmine rice, to serve

EQUIPMENT

- vegetable peeler
- rolling pin
- saucepan and lid
- tweezers
- chopping board
- knife
- bowl
- metal spoon
- large heavy-based saucepan
- wooden spoon
- ladle

1 Run your fingers over the fish to check for bones. If you find any, pick them out with your fingers or use a pair of tweezers.

2 Using a chopping board and a knife, cut the fish into large bite-size pieces and put in a bowl.

3 Cut the squash in half, scoop out the seeds using a metal spoon, and then cut the flesh into bite-size pieces. Cut the pak choi into same size pieces.

4 Heat the oil in a large saucepan and add the curry paste. It will start to sizzle—cook about 2 minutes, stirring continuously with a wooden spoon. Add the turmeric and stir a few seconds.

5 Pour in the coconut milk, fish stock, and fish sauce and add the superfine sugar, lemon grass, and lime leaves. Stir well and then bring up to a gentle simmer.

6 Add the squash and cook 12 minutes or until just cooked—you should be able to easily poke the squash with a knife.

7 Now add the fish, pak choi and half the fresh cilantro and cook 5 minutes, or until the fish is cooked.

8 Add more fish sauce and freshly ground black pepper to taste. Sprinkle over the remaining cilantro. Ladle the steamed rice into bowls and then top with the curry.

marinades

Fish, meat, and vegetables (see page 31) can all be marinated before being cooked. Marinades not only add flavor to the food, but can also help to tenderize meat before cooking. These are a few marinade ideas for lamb, chicken, and fish. Once you have all the ingredients together in a large bowl, mix well, and gently massage the marinade into the meat or fish with your fingers. Cover with plastic wrap and place in the refrigerator until you're ready to cook. The longer you leave the meat, the deeper the flavor it will have of the marinade. Overnight is often ideal, but a few hours will do—although if you are going to marinate fish in lemon juice, only leave the fish in the juice for 10 minutes or so because the juice will start to cook the fish. If you find the garlic too overpowering for the fish, simply remove the crushed cloves before you start to cook it.

You can use a pastry brush to brush any remaining marinade on to the meat and fish while cooking.

for approx. 1 lb cubed lamb or chicken

- juice of 1 lemon,1 small onion, sliced
- 5 tablespoons olive oil
- 1 tablespoons chopped fresh oregano
- 1–2 garlic cloves, peeled and crushed

Thread the marinated cubes of lamb or chicken on to metal or pre-soaked wooden skewers (see page 31). Place on the grill of a hot barbecue or underneath a hot broiler and turn occasionally until cooked through (see page 30, point 7). This should take around 20–25 minutes.

for 6 chicken drumsticks

- 2 tablespoons runny honey
- 1 tablespoons soy sauce
- ⅕ inch piece of fresh ginger. peeled and chopped
- ½ cup yogurt
- juice of ½ lemon
- 2 garlic cloves, peeled and chopped
- large pinch of paprika

Using oven gloves, place the marinated drumsticks in a roasting pan in an oven preheated to 400°F and cook for 30 minutes, or until cooked through (see page 44, point 4).

for 1 lb fresh cubed fish such as monkish

- handful of fresh chopped herbs
- 2 tablespoons olive oil
- juice of 1 lemon
- 2 inch piece of fresh ginger, peeled and chopped
- 1 tablespoon soy sauce
- 2 teaspoons sesame oil
- 1–2 garlic cloves, peeled and crushed
- 2 scallions, chopped

Thread the marinated cubes of monkish on to metal or pre-soaked wooden skewers (see page 31). Place on the grill of a hot barbecue or underneath a hot broiler and turn occasionally until just cooked (see page 12, point 5). This shouldn't take longer than a few minutes.

marinades

sticky spare ribs

SERVES 4

These are good fun to make and even more fun to eat!

YOU WILL NEED:

INGREDIENTS
- 1 garlic clove, peeled
- 2 tablespoons tomato paste
- 2 tablespoons dark brown sugar
- 2 tablespoons light soy sauce
- 1 tablespoons red wine vinegar
- 1 tablespoons honey
- 1 tablespoons vegetable oil
- 1 cup orange juice
- salt and freshly ground black pepper
- 20 uncooked pork spare ribs—approx 2 lbs)

EQUIPMENT
- knife
- garlic crusher
- medium bowl
- small whisk
- large roasting tin
- oven gloves
- wooden spoon

1 Turn the oven on to 350°F.

2 Crush the garlic in a garlic press and put into a bowl. Add the tomato paste, sugar, soy sauce, vinegar, honey, oil, and orange juice. Season with pepper and a pinch of salt, then whisk until it is smooth.

3 Lay the ribs in a roasting pan in a single layer. Pour over half the sauce. Turn the ribs to make sure they are completely covered.

4 Using oven gloves, put the ribs in the oven and cook 20 minutes, then take them out and give them a really good stir, and put back in the oven another 10 minutes. Use oven gloves to take them out of the oven again and pour over the remaining marinade. Give them another really good stir and put them back in the oven a further 15–20 minutes.

5 Using oven gloves, remove the roasting pan from the oven. These are delicious served with rice and salad.

marinades

pesto-marinated chicken drumsticks

SERVES 3

A few simple ingredients make a wonderful marinade. You can buy ready-made pesto from supermarkets and delis.

YOU WILL NEED:
INGREDIENTS
- 1 garlic clove, peeled
- 2 tablespoons pesto
- 2 tablespoons olive oil
- 2 tablespoons lemon juice
- salt and freshly ground black pepper
- 6 chicken drumsticks (approx 1 lb 10 oz)

EQUIPMENT
- garlic press
- large bowl
- spoon
- knife
- chopping board
- plastic wrap
- roasting pan
- oven gloves
- kitchen tongs

1 Using a garlic press, crush the garlic and put into a large bowl. Add the pesto, oil, and lemon juice. Season with salt and freshly ground black pepper. Mix together with a spoon.

2 Using a knife and a chopping board, carefully cut small slits into the chicken drumsticks without cutting all the way through to the bone.

3 Add the chicken drumsticks to the pesto mixture.

4 Using your clean hands, really massage the marinade into the chicken, making sure it coats the chicken thoroughly. Wash your hands. Cover the bowl with plastic wrap and leave the chicken to marinate in the refrigerator at least half an hour or longer if possible.

5 Turn on the oven to 400°F. Spoon the chicken and any juices into a roasting pan and, using oven gloves, put into the oven. Cook for 30 minutes or until cooked through (see page 44, point 4).

6 Lift the drumsticks out of the pan with tongs, leaving the fat in the pan.

using cutters

You can use pretty shaped cutters, such as hearts or flowers, to cut out cookies. They're great for themed parties, such as Christmas or Halloween.

Billy's raspberry and cocoa biscuits

MAKES 18–20

YOU WILL NEED:

INGREDIENTS
- ¾ stick butter
- ½ cup superfine sugar
- 1 cup all-purpose flour, plus extra for rolling out
- 3 tablespoons sweetened cocoa powder
- 18–20 raspberry flavor hard candies

EQUIPMENT
- 2 baking sheets
- baking parchment
- large bowl
- wooden spoon
- flour sifter
- knife
- rolling pin
- 2 inch and ⅝ inch cutters
- palette knife
- oven gloves
- wire rack
- large white plate

1   Turn on the oven to 350°F. Line 2 baking sheets with parchment.

2   Put the butter and sugar together in a large bowl and, using a wooden spoon, beat together until pale and creamy.

3   Sift the flour and cocoa powder into the butter and sugar mixture and stir to mix well, until it comes together to form a dough.

4   Sprinkle some flour on to your work surface. Cut the dough in half and roll half of it out until it is about ⅕ inch thick.

5   Ⓐ Using the large cutter, cut the dough into shapes of your choice. Using the smaller cutter, cut a hole in the centre of each shape. Use a palette knife to lift the shapes of dough on to the baking sheets—you may need to pop out the centers as you lift them.

6   Put a hard candy in the middle of each circle.

7   Using oven gloves, put the baking sheets into the oven and bake the cookie 6–8 minutes, or until cooked and slightly golden.

8   Using oven gloves, take the baking sheets out of the oven. Leave to cool slightly. Then lift off the cookies with a palette knife and leave to cool completely on a wire rack. They are quite brittle so be gentle. Serve the cookies on a white plate so the centers really stand out.

using cutters

Swedish gingerbread biscuits (pepparkakor)

MAKES 10

These cookies are traditionally made at Christmas in Sweden where it is common to make a gingerbread house, too. If you would like to hang your cookies on your Christmas tree, poke a hole in the top of each one before you cook the cookies, and when they are cool, frost them, and then thread some ribbon or string through the holes.

YOU WILL NEED:

INGREDIENTS

- small knob of butter, for greasing
- 1⅔ cups all-purpose flour, plus a little extra for rolling out
- 1½ level teaspoons bicarbonate of soda
- 1 level teaspoon ground ginger
- ½ level teaspoon cinnamon
- ½ level teaspoon ground cloves
- ½ stick butter
- ½ cup light brown sugar
- 1½ tablespoons golden or corn syrup
- ½ tablespoon molasses
- very finely grated zest of ½ orange

to decorate:

- ⅗ cup confectioners' sugar
- lemon juice or warm water
- currants

EQUIPMENT

- grater
- 3 baking sheets
- flour sifter and large bowl
- knife
- small bowl
- small whisk
- metal spoon
- plastic wrap
- rolling pin
- gingerbread man cutters
- palette knife and oven gloves
- wire rack
- small bowl
- spoon

1 Turn the oven to 375°F. Rub 3 baking sheets lightly with a small knob of butter.

2 Sift the flour, bicarbonate of soda, ginger, cinnamon, and cloves into a large bowl. Cut the butter into small pieces and add to the bowl. Rub it in with your fingertips until the mixture looks like breadcrumbs.

3 Crack the egg into a small bowl, add the sugar, syrup, molasses, and orange zest. Mix well with a small whisk. Use a metal spoon to stir this mixture into the flour. As it starts to come together, use your hands to knead it into a ball of dough.

4 Sprinkle a little flour on to your work surface then tip the dough out and knead it a minute or 2 until it is smooth. Wrap it in plastic wrap and leave to rest in the refrigerator 10 minutes.

5 Sprinkle a little more flour over the work surface and, using your rolling pin, roll the dough out to about ⅕ inch thick. Dip your cookie cutters into flour then cut out as many shapes as you can. Use a palette knife to carefully lift the cookies on to the baking sheets. Gather up any spare dough and knead again into a ball. Roll it out and cut out more cookies and place on the baking sheets.

6 Use oven gloves to put the baking sheets into the oven and cook the cookies 6–10 minutes, or until golden brown.

7 Using oven gloves, take the baking sheets out of the oven. Let them cool for a few minutes, then lift them carefully on to a wire rack, and leave them to cool completely.

8 Now make the frosting: sift the icing sugar into a bowl. Gradually add a little lemon juice or water and mix until you have a thick smooth paste. You can use just white frosting, or if you prefer, add a tiny drop of food coloring and mix well. Use the frosting to decorate the cookies and pop currants on for "eyes" and "buttons." Leave the frosting to set.

fermentation

During fermentation in a drink, the yeast feeds on the sugar in the liquid to produce carbon dioxide gas. This would normally escape into the air, but if the liquid is bottled before fermentation is complete, some of the gas is trapped inside, which makes the drink fizzy.

ginger beer

MAKES 5 PINTS

YOU WILL NEED:
INGREDIENTS
- 1 cup granulated sugar
- 2½ tablespoons cream of tartar
- 2½ tablespoons ground ginger
- 5 pints boiling water
- 1 oz dried yeast

EQUIPMENT
- 2 large bowls
- long-handled wooden spoon
- strainer
- muslin or clean dish towel
- large ladle
- tumbler
- 4 washed and rinsed EZ-Cap ("flip cap") beer bottles, each should hold 1 pint. It is essential to use the correct ginger beer bottles with metal clip lids. These are available from good wine and beer making supply stores. Ordinary wine and beer bottles are not strong enough to contain gas and they may explode!

1 Put the sugar, cream of tartar, and ginger into a large bowl.

2 Carefully pour in the boiling water—you may need an adult to help you with this. Use a wooden spoon to mix it all together until the sugar is completely dissolved.

3 Leave the bowl until the mixture is at blood temperature—if you dip a finger into the liquid, it should feel as warm as your finger, but not hotter.

4 Add the dried yeast and stir for a couple of minutes until the yeast is completely dissolved.

5 Set a strainer over another large bowl. Line the strainer with a piece of muslin or a clean dish towel.

6 **A** Using a ladle, fill the strainer with the ginger beer mixture and leave to strain through the material into the bowl. It will trickle through very slowly so be patient and go back to the bowl every half an hour or so to fill up the sieve.

7 When all the liquid has been strained, remove the strainer. Use a clean tumbler to dip into the bowl and fill up the ginger beer bottles.

8 Fix the lids on firmly. If you have spilt any liquid down the sides of the bottles, rinse it off and dry them. Leave the bottles in a cool dark place for 24 hours.

9 Be careful when you open the bottles, because the beer will be very fizzy and the mixture may spurt out quite quickly.

melting chocolate

Chocolate is melted in a bowl over a saucepan of simmering water. Be very careful when you melt it not to get it too hot—just keep the water simmering gently rather than boiling.

hot chocolate drink

MAKES 4 MUGS

Instead of cocoa powder, you could try sprinkling grated chocolate or a pinch of ground cinnamon over the top. Alternatively, leave the hot chocolate to cool and serve over ice or with ice cream.

YOU WILL NEED:
INGREDIENTS
- 3½ oz good quality bittersweet or milk chocolate (or use half of each)
- 2⅓ cups whole milk
- ⅓ cup heavy cream, whipped to soft peak stage
- 8 marshmallows (optional)
- a little cocoa, for dusting

EQUIPMENT
- 2 saucepans
- large bowl
- oven gloves
- wooden spoon
- whisk
- small pitcher and 4 mugs
- spoon

OTHER THINGS TO DO WITH MELTED CHOCOLATE
- ✔ scoop little balls of ice cream and stick a small lollipop stick into the middle of each ball, then freeze until solid. Dip the balls of ice cream into melted chocolate and then freeze again until set
- ✔ half dip cookies or snackjacks into melted chocolate
- ✔ half dip large nuts, such as Brazil nuts, or pieces of mango into melted chocolate

1 Half fill a saucepan with water and bring up to a gentle simmer. Break the chocolate into small pieces and put into a bowl. Rest the bowl in the pan so that the bowl sits above the simmering water but doesn't touch it.

2 **A** Leave about 4 minutes until the chocolate has melted. Take the pan off the heat and using oven gloves take the bowl off the saucepan. Give the chocolate a gentle stir with a wooden spoon until it is smooth and glossy.

3 Put the milk into a saucepan and bring just up to boiling point without letting it boil. Remove from the heat. Add a little of the milk to the chocolate, stirring constantly with a whisk until you have a thick paste. Pour over the rest of the milk and whisk until the mixture is slightly frothy.

4 Carefully pour the mixture into a pitcher, then pour it into the mugs. Spoon the whipped cream on top of the hot chocolate. Put 2 marshmallows on the top of each mug and sprinkle over a little cocoa powder.

A

caramel

Caramel is sugar that has melted into a liquid that is then cooked to a golden brown color. It can be used to top desserts, such as crème brûlée, or, once hard, it can be crushed up and added to desserts such as ice cream. The temperature at which sugar starts to caramelize is very hot— 325°F – if you have a sugar thermometer use it in this recipe, asking an adult to help you. If, by accident, any of the caramel splashes on to your hand (or anywhere else), quickly put your hand into cold water.

honeycomb

MAKES AROUND 30 PIECES

This is particularly delicious sprinkled over ice cream, or smash into large chunks and then half dip each piece into melted chocolate.

YOU WILL NEED:

INGREDIENTS
- small knob of butter, for greasing
- 4 heaped teaspoons bicarbonate of soda
- 1 ½ cups granulated sugar
- 6 tablespoons golden or corn syrup

EQUIPMENT
- approx. 6 x 11 inch deep-sided rectangular roasting pan
- dish towel
- small bowl
- whisk
- heavy-based deep-sided saucepan
- wooden spoon
- oven gloves
- rolling pin

1 Rub the base and sides of the pan with a little butter. This will make it easier for you to take the honeycomb out of the pan.

2 Put a dish towel on the work surface. Put the bicarbonate of soda into a small bowl, next to the dish towel, and have your whisk ready for when you take the pan off the heat.

3 Put the sugar and golden or corn syrup into a large saucepan and mix together well with a wooden spoon.

4 Put the pan on to the hob over a gentle heat. Asking an adult to help you, stir constantly until the sugar and syrup have completely melted, then turn the heat up a little until the mixture is golden and bubbling—don't let it get any darker or it will taste burned. It will take about 4–6 minutes from the moment you put the pan on the heat to the time you take it off.

5 Using your oven gloves, take the pan off the heat, asking an adult to help you, and put it on the dish towel. Remove the wooden spoon.

6 Sprinkle the bicarbonate of soda over the mixture and whisk it in quickly but firmly—it will immediately start to bubble up and increase in volume.

7 Holding the pan with your oven gloves, carefully pour the hot mixture into the prepared pan—get an adult to help you with this bit.

8 Leave the honeycomb to set at least 3 hours, then use a rolling pin to smash it into bits. Store in an airtight container.

Index